Hunting the Great Plains

John Barsness

Mountain Press Publishing Company
Missoula, Montana

Library of Congress Cataloging in Publication Data

Barsness, John.
  Hunting the Great Plains.

  Includes index.
  1.   Hunting — Great Plains.   I.   Title.
SK45.B37   799.2'978   79-22096
ISBN 0-87842-117-3

For My Father
I wish he could be here

Acknowledgments

Many thanks to the game departments of the plains states and provinces mentioned in this book for their information and time; to Norm Strung for advice and photos; to *Sports Afield* magazine, and especially Fred Kesting, for permission to use parts of an article of mine they published; and most especially to Ben Burshia, for teaching me most of what I know about hunting in the wide-open spaces.

Contents

Introduction vii

BIG GAME

One: Whitetailed Deer 1
Two: Pronghorn 13
Three: Mule Deer 25
Four: Other Big Game 32
Five: Plains Rifles & Guns 34

UPLAND GAME

Six: Sage Grouse 51
Seven: Sharptailed Grouse,
        Greater & Lesser Prairie Chicken 58
Eight: Hungarian Partridge 66
Nine: Ringnecked Pheasant 73
Ten: Bobwhite Quail & Scaled Quail 83
Eleven: Wild Turkey 91
Twelve: Open-Country Dogs For Upland Game 99
Thirteen: Open-Country Shotguns & Shooting 109

MIGRATORY BIRDS

Fourteen: Ducks & Geese 125
Fifteen: Mourning Dove 135
Sixteen: Other Migratory Birds 140
Seventeen: Small Game 143
Eighteen: Vehicles & Camping 149
Index 161

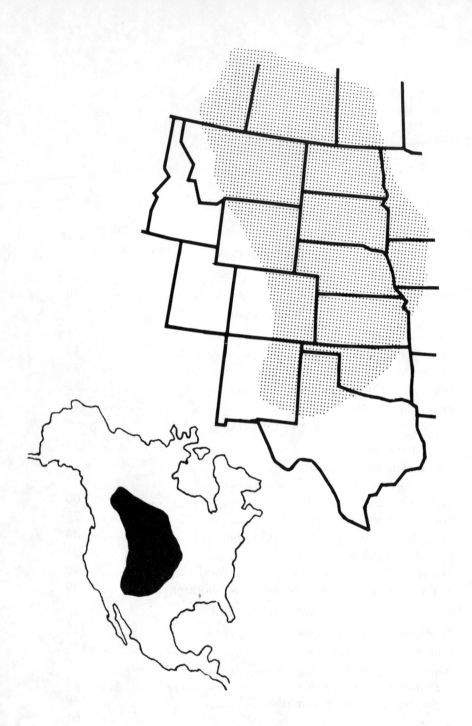

Introduction

When you first approach from a distance, the upper branches of the cottonwood trees are all that are visible across the tan-green prairie hills. It isn't until you draw nearer, walking along the edge of a deep hollow created by the spring's erosion and looking down to see sixty-foot trees, that you start to realize what is hidden there.

The place is called Ericson's, though no one by that name or any other has lived there for a quarter of a century. To me, that small spot on the prairie of northeastern Montana is the essence of the wide-open spaces that stretch across the center of our continent. Ericson's is an oasis created by man and nature, in the midst of the grama-grass prairie. The old foundation is all that's left of the house; above the spring hollow are rows of man-planted trees serving to break the constant northeasterly wind. Thick thigh-high wild rosebushes cover the slopes leading down into the hollow, and in the deep bottom are patches of serviceberry, wild currant, and wild raspberry, along with plum bushes and crabapple trees planted by Ericson, whoever he was. Tall broad leaves of wild horseradish surround the grassy openings of the bottom, and the smell of wild mint is everywhere.

The cottonwood trees, perhaps three dozen, surround the spring's seep. If you walk between their thick trunks, stepping on clumps of high ground, you can sometimes startle the great horned owl that lives in one of the higher trees, and he'll float through the crowded branches, somehow finding room to spread his broad wings.

If spring frosts haven't killed the berry crop, there'll be game birds around, either in the windbreaks or in the thickets. Hungarian partridge and sharptailed grouse will flush loudly and sail over the hill, and mourning doves will flutter out of the cottonwoods. Sometimes, as you walk down into the thicket, you'll hear the crash of a deer. They always wait until you are down there, in the bottom, before they go, and they leave without being seen.

The life of the prairie is concentrated around that spring and can be followed for several miles below the cottonwoods along a small stream that winds through a coulee filled with short brush and occasional taller thickets. The drainage then enters the dry creek bottom of a large valley which in turn drains into the Poplar River a dozen miles to the east. The coulees and dry creeks and rivers are the veins and arteries of the prairies and plains, dendritic patterns carrying the lifeblood of the land — water. Down in the spring hollow of Ericson's you can feel that life beginning, are aware of the vitality of the prairie all around you.

Strangely, it is also the scarcity of water on the prairies and plains that is the basis of that vitality. The northern grasslands rarely receive much more than a foot of precipitation a year — the hotter southern grasslands perhaps six inches more — and the minerals and nutrients that would be washed through the soil by a greater amount of rainfall stay near the surface. The various prairie plants — grasses, forbs, shrubs — send their roots to different depths in the topsoil, extracting different minerals, flourishing during different seasons. The result is a complex "layering" of the soil and an adaptability that allows the upper, living layer of the prairie to survive Saskatchewan winters, Texas droughts, or roaring, wind-driven fires. I have seen a ten-acre swath of grama grass burned only the week before turn intensely green almost overnight with the touch of an afternoon's rain.

Those mineral-rich prairie grasses once supported the greatest wildlife show this continent has ever seen. As many as 60 million buffalo grazed from Texas to Saskatchewan; as recently as 150 years ago elk were common in the riverbottoms of South Dakota and Nebraska; bighorn sheep clambered over the breaks and badlands of the Dakotas and eastern Montana; pronghorn, wild turkeys, prairie grouse, wolves, deer, grizzly bears — all existed in the thousands and even millions across the "Great American Desert." It was no accident that the plains Indians were the most powerful tribes. The vast herds of game allowed them to prosper, and the lush grasses enabled individual Indian villages to graze herds of several thousand horses.

Early fur trappers and explorers were intensely aware that the plains were the most bountiful portion of the west. The men of the Lewis and Clark expedition ate plentifully while they crossed the prairies, hunters in the party easily supplying the one buffalo, two elk, or several deer required each day to feed 30 hard-working men. Once the expedition entered the Rockies, it found little game; the journals of the two leaders constantly note a scarcity of even smaller game animals. They also noticed that the mountain Indian bands were small in number, and their members not as tall or well-built as the well-fed plains Indians.

The westward tumble of "civilization" eventually doomed the herds of buffalo, the vast flocks of sage grouse, the elk of the open country. By the 1880's, most of the game was gone. Theodore Roosevelt, who ranched in the badlands of western North Dakota during that decade, noted that elk and buffalo were virtually extinct in the area, and that even deer and pronghorn were in short supply, though he hunted all four animals. He also hunted the badlands bighorn sheep, the Audubon subspecies, and falsely predicted that the bighorn, because of the rugged hills it inhabited, would survive long after the deer were gone — the Audubon bighorn became extinct in the early part of this century. By the 1920's, cowboys were riding miles just to tell their companions they'd seen a real, live deer, and naturalists were predicting the extinction of the sage grouse, prairie chicken, and pronghorn.

The past half-century, though, has seen a remarkable restoration. While we'll never see "buffalo" wolves or plains grizzlies again, there are unendangered, stable numbers of almost all the other plains game, and tremendous populations of some. Pronghorn have increased from only 20,000 at the turn of the century to over half a million today. Whitetailed deer are common over the prairies. Sage grouse and prairie chickens, which seemed headed for extinction, can be hunted in several states, and there are even small populations of buffalo, elk and bighorn sheep that allow limited hunting in certain areas of the plains, though they are hunted far more often with cameras than with guns.

The plains and prairies have changed. Much of the grama, bluestem, and buffalo grass has been replaced by man's grasses: wheat, corn, barley, and oats. Buffalo have been supplanted by Angus and Hereford. The productivity of the plains has been changed from nature's to man's. Some animals, like the prairie chicken and mule deer, have been reduced in number by agriculture's alteration of nature, while others, like the bobwhite quail and whitetailed deer, have thrived on man's changes of the land.

We'll never see again the vast black herds of buffalo or be able to hunt elk in the Missouri riverbottoms of the corn belt, but the plains and prairies today offer as great a variety of game as any area of North America. On a single fall day in eastern Montana a few years ago, I saw mule deer, whitetailed deer, pronghorn, sharptailed and sage grouse, Hungarian partridge, pheasant, Canada geese, and mallard, teal and pintail ducks. In a hike of two miles in the same area I've traversed swampy tule marshes, thick hardwood timber, open grasslands, brushy coulees, and eroded badlands. It is that incredible variety of both wildlife and country that makes me wish I could be, at this moment, under an eastern Montana sky.

BIG GAME

This northern plains deer, a Dakota whitetail, displays the heavier, shorter-tined antlers of that subspecies. This buck was taken as it jumped from a brushy coulee in northeastern Montana.

Chapter One:
Whitetailed Deer

Odocoileus virginianus

The hunter was in the middle of his second ham-and-cheese sandwich when he saw the eye. It was a large brown eye, and it was looking at him steadily from perhaps 30 feet away, through a tiny space between the branches of a buffaloberry thicket. The hunter's sandwich stopped, poised in mid-air. The eye blinked. The hunter blinked. The eye suddenly disappeared, and the near-by brush started waving violently. The sound of a large animal crashing through the thicket smothered the hunter's low curse as he dropped the sandwich and ran for his pickup, parked 50 feet away. He grabbed his rifle from its rack and bolted a cartridge into the chamber, whirling in the direction of the animal's flight. He was just in time to see the heavy antlers and whipping white tail of a big deer disappear over a nearby ridge.

The hunter sighed, then dejectedly replaced the rifle in the rack. He laughed wryly as he walked to where he'd dropped his sandwich. Picking up scattered pieces of bread and ham and cheese, he flicked off a few bits of grass and dirt, but a closer look led him to toss the whole mess into the brush.

1

Only ten minutes before, the hunter had thrown several rocks into that buffaloberry patch, hoping to drive out any deer that might be bedded there. When nothing had emerged, he'd decided to sit in the warm Montana sun and eat his lunch. The big buck had ignored the rocks and sat quietly within sandwich-tossing distance while the hunter munched, not bolting until sure he had been seen. Typical of the prairie whitetail, this deer was just as smart as whitetails in other parts of the country and not an easier to outwit just because he lived in wide-opened spaces.

Most hunters think of whitetails as creatures of the forest and brush, living in tangles of northern hardwood forest, southern swamp, or Texas brush, successfully pursued only by those willing to sit for hours in an elevated stand, or to track a buck through a foot of snow. But the fact is that the whitetail is the top big game animal in every type of terrain south of the Canadian tundra and east of the Rockies, including the flatlands of our continent's midsection.

There are three main subspecies of prairie whitetail hunted on the grasslands extending from the southern prairie provinces of Canada to the Panhandle of Texas. They are all large deer, differing as far as the hunter is concerned only in where they're found; the actual differences not usually discernible to the non-taxonomic eye. The big buck that lay perusing our hunter was a specimen of the Dakota whitetail, which ranges from southern Canada south to northern Nebraska, and from the eastern Dakotas to eastern Montana. South and east into Oklahoma is the range of the Kansas whitetail, a deer that has perhaps disappeared in its pure strain because its range has been planted with other deer and also partially invaded by bordering subspecies. The grasslands of eastern Colorado and the western parts of southern Nebraska, Kansas, and Oklahoma are occupied by the Texas whitetail, which on the prairie is usually a large deer, but which in some areas can be much smaller. The Texas deer roams to the southern limits of the grasslands, which include parts of the Texas Panhandle and extreme eastern New Mexico.

All these deer are more widespread than they were prior to the cultivation of the prairies and plains. Whitetails can get along with man much more readily than either mule deer or pronghorn antelope, the other two principal plains and prairie big game animals; whitetails are found in many areas that were formerly

2

the domain of mule deer and pronghorns. My wife's grandfather, Ben Burshia, has hunted deer in northeastern Montana since around 1910; he says that there were practically no whitetails in that country when he was growing up, even in the riverbottoms — almost all the deer were mule deer. Today at least 95% of the deer in that region are whitetails.

The whitetail adapts readily to open-country life, but it is still tied to brushy cover. The cottonwood-willow vegetation along prairie rivers harbors many whitetail, and further out on the open prairie, little patches of brush and timber are prime spots for whitetails to bed and browse, though the open terrain has resulted in slightly different lives for the deer. It has long been accepted that whitetails are born, live, and die in a relatively small area — perhaps a square mile. However, from my observations (and those of many others) I'd say that while most of the prairie whitetails are born in the timbered riverbottoms of the plains, many — perhaps most — don't spend their entire lives there and may "migrate" 10 or even 20 miles seasonally. There are several reasons for this. One is that the wetness of riverbottoms in spring produces insects that literally drive the deer from the timber. Bucks are the first to scatter into more open country, followed by does with fawns. Winter, especially on the northern prairie, will eventually drive most of these deer back to the protection of timber, but during summer and fall there are many deer living in scattered patches of brush that edge the coulees and draws of the open country.

Another reason for the deer being so common in open country is population. The whitetail is a cover-oriented animal, preferring thick brush; he would rather lie still or hide than run from danger. When their numbers increase, the deer are forced into every available patch of cover, and the whitetail population continues to grow over many parts of the West. In Montana, Fish & Game Department biologists claim the whitetail are vastly underharvested compared to mule deer. Either-sex and two-deer seasons are held in many Western states for whitetail because there are too many deer for the cover available.

The open-country deer are easier to find than the timber deer, just because there is so little available habitat. Imagine a stretch of gently rolling, grassy hills veined with dry creeks and draws. Now try to imagine a whitetailed deer lying on top of one of those naked hills, taking in the sun's full force; it would be like trying to imagine John Wayne in drag. Even open-country whitetails like brush, and every little patch of chokecherry, buffalo-berry, or ash, and each stand of half-a-dozen cottonwoods may hold deer. Perhaps the ideal whitetail bedding spot in open country is a brush patch at least 20 to 30 feet wide, on the side of a steep, short coulee bounded by two sharp ridges. Such a spot offers deer plenty of cover and several escape routes. If approached from above, a deer runs down the coulee and around one of the ridge-points. If approached from below, it runs out of the top of the coulee. It can run over either ridge if approached from one of the ridge-tops.

It would seem that a deer bedded in such a spot would be almost invulnerable — and it would be, except for one flaw in the whitetail's nature. When a hunter surprises a whitetail in a patch of brush surrounded by open country, the deer's love of cover often overcomes its urge to flee. The deer remains still and tries to stay hidden, often refusing to leave cover.

Open-country whitetail hunters often take advantage of this trait. The basic method for hunting whitetails on the plains and prairies of the Dakotas, eastern Montana, and Nebraska, is to approach such spots from a direction offering a reasonable shot if the deer jumps, then to toss rocks into the brush. It sounds crude, but it works. It's exciting, too; tossing rocks into a good patch of whitetail cover ranks right up there with walking up behind a tightly-locked pointer in good quail country, but comparing the flush of a big whitetail buck with that of a covey of quail is like comparing a sonic boom with the backfiring of a truck.

On one occasion Ben Burshia and I were hunting the edges of a big wheatland plateau in northeastern Montana, near my former home in Poplar. We'd tossed rocks into every brush patch on the sides of that plateau except one — and Ben warned me that it was the best spot of all. We parked the pickup behind a ridge and walked quietly to a high undercut hill above the brush patch. I could feel my pulse pounding as I picked up several fist-sized stones; when Ben signaled he was ready, I fired a rock as hard as I could toward the sprawling 50-foot patch of chokecherry and ash that lay below us, covering the base of the opposite slope. The rock snapped through the brush, and before it rolled to a stop, another crash began. The brush waved, and a young six-point buck leaped from the edge of the thicket and sprinted for the ridge-top. It didn't get far, though — Ben's ancient Model 70 went bang and the buck collapsed. At the shot, another part of the brush began waving, and I saw a tall, wide set of antlers sweeping above the gray brush. A cartridge was already in the .270's chamber, and I pointed the rifle at the opposite hillside, anticipating the deer's flight path, but the buck fooled me. He came out the the brush straight toward us, trying to run under the lip of the cutbank we were standing on. Hurriedly I jerked the rifle down and found him in the 4x scope. At the shot he swerved sharply; at a second shot he stumbled, ran 20 feet, then fell. Another three bounds would have put him out of sight below us.

That big buck had 10 points and a 19″ spread — and he had acted as unpredictably as do really big bucks anywhere. Almost every time I've jumped a big prairie whitetail with smaller deer, the big one has taken a different escape route from the other deer. Once Ben and I jumped six deer from a small stand of cottonwoods in a long coulee. There were three does, two small bucks, and one real trophy. The five smaller deer ran up the sides of the coulee, and I killed one of the young bucks, but the big one headed straight down the bottom of the coulee, directly away from us, and we never glimpsed him again.

Large bucks usually pick the most invulnerable spots. There's one coulee I've hunted every year for the past five, a living example of the ideal spot for a large buck. It is a short, deep coulee bounded by two ridges, and one side of the coulee is covered with buffaloberry. In those five years my companions and I have jumped eight or ten deer there, six of them large bucks. We collected only two, but both were big ten-pointers, one just over 200 pounds and the other just under. The best strategy for such spots is to post a hunter near the deer's likely escape route — usually the ridge-point farthest from the brush — and have another hunter try to drive the deer out of the brush. The odds are about equal for either hunter getting a shot.

Big whitetail bucks are also found in a type of plains habitat usually associated with mule deer: badlands. I'm not talking about those tourist-attraction stretches of badlands in the Dakotas, but about small sections of eroded semi-desert that can be found almost anywhere in the open plains. In some regions really big whitetail bucks have taken a cue from the train robbers and horse thieves of the 19th-century West, realizing they can find peace and quiet amidst gumbo buttes and sandstone cliffs, mainly because most people don't often venture into the badlands. There's a big stretch of such country on the south side of the Missouri River in northeastern Montana that holds some of the biggest whitetail bucks I've ever seen. An acquaintance came by my house one fall with a whitetail he'd taken a mile back in those barren hills. The massive antlers on that buck spread an even two feet — and this was the smaller of two bucks my friend said he'd jumped from a patch of stumpy juniper trees.

The only requirement missing from a deer's life in that country is water — often there isn't any at all. I've followed deer trails through those twisting hills and am sure that those big bucks are willing to travel several miles each night down to the Missouri to get a drink. That's how much they value their privacy.

Badlands areas are perhaps the only kind of plains habitat that a whitetail hunter can effectively hunt with binoculars or by trail watching. Sparse cover, though, makes the deer nervous, and a hunter who constantly skylines himself and doesn't heed the wind will see very few badlands whitetails. Watching the few waterholes in those regions can pay off; a cousin of mine took a nice buck last fall when it came to drink at a stock dam on the edge of a small section of badlands. By any method, however, badlands bucks are tough to hunt, but they're also big. I'd rate badlands areas as the best bets for someone who wants a trophy open-country whitetail.

Hunters who pursue big whitetails in other parts of the country often concentrate on the rut, knowing that big deer are less wary then, but I haven't found the rut to be much help on the prairies. In open country, whitetails seem to realize they're more vulnerable, restricting breeding activities to night for the most part. That deer tend to move around more during the rut can work to a hunter's advantage. Good open-country whitetail spots are often miles apart, but during the rut, a spot that holds no deer today may hold several tomorrow. However, deer also seem to be wilder under the influence of the breeding moon, not waiting for a hunter to roust them from their beds. Prior to the rut, big bucks will be the hardest to drive from cover. Many times I've tossed a dozen rocks into a patch of brush before a big buck would leave, and they're always the last out of the brush patch if several deer are jumped at once; but during the rut, the mere appearance of a hunter may send a big whitetail out of his bed and over the hill.

The whitetail that live in the Western riverbottoms, on the other hand, are typical forest deer, with two exceptions: the "forests" they inhabit are cottonwood timber and willow thickets, and there are more deer in the Western riverbottoms than in the Eastern hardwood timber. This is especially true the farther west you go — Montana, Wyoming, eastern Colorado, western Nebraska, and even the Panhandles of Texas and Oklahoma all have substantial populations of mule deer, and much of the time hunting pressure is diverted to the "easier" mule deer. In many Western plains areas, whitetail have increased their range, particularly in the last 20 to 30 years, but many local hunters who grew up hunting open-country mulies, and never really learned how to hunt timber whitetails, are still reluctant to venture into the riverbottoms after those "other" deer.

Part of the reason for large numbers of whitetail in these areas has been an increase in human activity, strange as that may sound. Many thickets were just overgrown wastelands, as far as deer were concerned, before men started chopping, burning, and clearing the land for fields. Every new field and every new road produced more "edge" to remaining forests and thickets, creating transitional zones where thick, essentially sterile forest with little deer food gave way to clearings with the low shrubbery where deer thrive.

Thus there are many Western cottonwood stands that are actually over-full of whitetail. Many Western states which limit mule deer hunting to bucks-only have either-sex whitetail hunting because there are too many riverbottom deer.

One fall day about three or four years ago, five friends and I hunted a stretch of the Yellowstone River in Montana. The standard technique was to post three of us at the end of a strip of timber or at the end of an island we could wade to and to have the other three hunters drive the deer toward the standers. We saw about two dozen deer in one morning, including four or five bucks with what would be mounting-size antlers in the East, and took two of those deer. On another occasion, in the same area, three bucks with antler spans of over 20" were taken in the same morning.

The nature of those riverbottoms makes them ideal for the

7

stand-and-drive technique. The timber is primarily in strips paralleling the river, and is further divided by roads and fields, creating little "islands" of cover. The deer either have to sit tight or break through an opening somewhere, instead of pulling the sneak maneuvers they're capable of in larger stretches of timber. And because they haven't been hunted much, they aren't as apt to sit still and let hunters go by, as do more sophisticated deer in harder-hunted areas.

I don't mean to imply that every Western riverbottom is alive with Boone & Crockett trophies just waiting to be harvested by some hunter willing to take a day off from the carpet factory. These deer must be hunted just like whitetails anywhere — skillfully and carefully. But numbers make it easier.

Another technique that a friend of mine tried for the first time last season worked well. Involving two or three hunters, it can be worked effectively by smaller parties. The hunters spread out, perhaps 100 yards apart, at one end of a patch of timber. Fully realizing there is no quiet way to sneak up on a whitetail deer through a three-inch floor of cottonwood leaves, the middle hunter (if there are three) sneaks forward for three minutes, then stops. The other two hunters, who've been watching their Timexes, then start forward at a prearranged time. They walk for five minutes, ending up just ahead of the first hunter's position, and stop. The middle hunter then walks for five minutes. What is created is a see-sawing line of advance. If a deer is jumped by a moving hunter it stands a good chance of running into one of the standers, and curious deer will often try to double back to get a look at what scared them. My friend had just finished one of his five-minute walks and was standing, waiting, when a buck stepped out of the timber 50 feet ahead, looking both ways like a person crossing the street. My friend waited until the deer looked the other way before he raised his rifle and filled his tag.

The individual hunter in one of these riverbottoms would be well advised to take a stand, preferably in a tree, but even ground-level stands will work if the hunter's outline is broken by branches. The best time to try this is during the rut, which in most northern states begins in the first part of November and runs through early December. Further south it begins two to three weeks earlier. Bucks will be moving around at any time of day, and if you find a spot overlooking two good trails or can locate a

8

breeding scrape, the chances are good that you'll collect something other than boredom.

During the peak of the rut on the Yellowstone, I was helping direct two North Dakota hunters to some good deer hunting. We had just finished standing at the end of an island during one drive and were crossing the river above an iced-over section on our way to the driving area, when one of the hunters started yelling. "Hey, hey, hey!' he shouted, pointing behind us. There, on the glare ice of the river, was a mid-size whitetail buck mincing along almost on tiptoe as he tried to maintain his balance on the ice. At the shout, the deer tried to scramble off the frozen river. For a moment he looked like a cartoon character as his legs flailed in vain on the frictionless ice; then his pounding hooves broke the thin layer, and he splashed into two feet of water. The two hunters sat down, readying their .243's, and I truly believe they would have shot the buck right there if I hadn't shouted: "Jesus Christ, wait till he gets to shore!" The buck was plunging forward, making slow headway toward the island, and I certainly didn't want to wade into knee-high icewater to drag him out. With the front of his body up on the ice, the buck scrambled with his front hooves, trying to climb out of the water. As soon as one hind hoof would get on the edge of the ice, it would break again, but he was slowly crashing toward shore, like an animate ice-breaker. Finally he broke through to shallow water and stumbled exhausted onto land where one of the Dakotans shot him.

During the peak of his yearly love life, even a really large buck is apt to forget what he's learned about survival. Down in Texas, they "rattle up" bucks during the rut by pounding a couple of antlers together to simulate a fight. Whitetail are territorial animals, especially during the rut, and the sound of a deer battle will often convince a nearby buck that rivals have invaded his little patch of cottonwood, and he will come running to investigate. Why this technique is common in Texas and nowhere else, I can't say. Some hunters theorize that it takes a high concentration of bucks to make it work. In an area of low deer density you may be wasting your time trying to rattle up a buck because none may be near or the deer may be less adamant about defending their territories. But many Western riverbottoms certainly hold an excess of deer, and I can't explain why the few people (including myself) who've tried rattling on lonely islands haven't had any

9

success. Perhaps we don't have enough faith. If you want to try it, however, most expert rattlers say to do it on a calm day (so the deer can't circle downwind and catch your scent) in camouflage clothing, hidden near a clearing. Ideally a location near a scrape should be chosen, though it's not necessary. Most rattlers say to rattle hard for perhaps half a minute at most, then wait. If nothing shows up in 15 minutes, try another spot. As I said, I don't know anyone who's successfully rattled up northern deer, but probably that's because so few people have tried this technique. There are certainly enough deer in some areas to make it work.

Where to Go

At the present time, Saskatchewan (which is the best northern trophy deer country) is closed to non-Canadian whitetail hunters, but those north-of-the-border hunters looking for a big buck should look to the southeastern part of the province, just north of the U.S. border. Hunt units 7, 9, and 16 had the largest harvests during recent years. The extreme southwestern corner of Manitoba also holds a few large deer, as does the northeastern and north-central part of North Dakota. All these areas, I must emphasize, are trophy deer areas, but hunting is also good in Saskatchewan throughout the southern half of the province, and in western North Dakota. And tropies can turn up anywhere.

Eastern Montana is full of whitetail. The northeastern corner is probably the best all-around whitetail habitat, but any of the riverbottoms throughout the eastern two-thirds of the state are overrun with deer. The farther you travel from the northeastern corner, the more mule deer you find in the hills and the more whitetail in the riverbottoms.

South Dakota also has good whitetail hunting, with the Black Hills foothills and the half of the state east of the Missouri River having the largest harvests. The biggest deer usually come from the Black Hills region, but big corn-country bucks are also taken from the corn belt in the southeastern portion of the state. The plains part of the state west of the Missouri (excluding the Black Hills) is about evenly divided between whitetail and mule deer, and the whitetail are usually in the creek and riverbottoms.

Wyoming and Nebraska share the Black Hills foothills with South Dakota, and many trophies have come from this region.

10

The Powder River bottoms in the northeast and the Bighorn Mountain foothills in the north-central area are also good Wyoming whitetail areas. In Nebraska the eastern third of the state, which is primarily agricultural country, is good, as is western Iowa, just across the Missouri River. This area, like southeastern South Dakota, is part of the corn belt and deer are especially fond of the strips of cover between riverbottom corn fields.

Whitetail in Kansas are most abundant in riverbottoms of the western part of the state and in the eastern corn belt. Eastern Colorado's creek bottoms also harbor whitetail, but hunting is only fair.

Texas' plains whitetail are primarily found in the northeastern corner of the Panhandle and in a few counties just south of the main Panhandle. This country, along with the eastern edge of New Mexico, is actually better mule deer country, and the whitetail are scarce, though by no means unhuntable by people that know the areas. The Texas area south of the Panhandle is perhaps the best for open-country whitetail, with most counties having two or three-deer limits, as opposed to the one-whitetail limit in the northeastern counties.

Pronghorn are the last of the truly plains big game commonly found in North America. Like most open-country big game animals, their main line of defense is their remarkable eyesight. The author took this buck after careful searching with binoculars and a cautious stalk – and the shot was still over 200 yards.

Chapter Two: Pronghorn

Antilocapra americana

We had first seen the band of 22 pronghorn the evening before. We'd beached the boat on a small island that rose above a mile-wide bay, and I'd scrambled to the top, through sagebrush and yucca. At the crest I'd knelt behind a tall sagebrush and used binoculars to scan the shoreline half-a-mile to the west. It was too far, even with the glasses, to see if any bucks were in the band, but it was mid-October, the middle of the pronghorn breeding season, and I was sure that there would be at least one good-sized buck in the herd.

We were at the island again, before daybreak the next morning, and I stepped in my footprints of the day before as I walked to the top. About 20 of the small, light-colored dots were no longer visible, having wandered over a hill in the night, but to the south two pronghorn still stood out against the gray-green of the sagebrush.

I trotted back down to the boat, and we circled wide, away from the island, until the two white dots disappeared behind a sandstone point. About 15 minutes later we beached the boat 300 yards from the end of that point, and I loaded the magazine of my rifle and started walking along the narrow beach. The sun was

13

just coming over the hills behind my right shoulder, red-orange with the intensity of a badlands sunrise, and I could feel my pulse quicken, involuntarily.

Nearing the point I got down on all fours and crawled around the base of a small sandstone cliff. Two pronghorn were feeding, heads down, only 200 yards away. Just as I eased the rifle up and looked through the scope at the larger of the two, it raised its head. It was a buck, his curving black horns contrasting with pale underbody and tan sides.

My elbows were dug solidly into the sand — the only problem was my heart; it pounded crazily, seeming to be apart from me. I held my breath, concentrating, and at the sound of the shot the buck disappeared into the sage. The startled doe, confused by the echoes of the shot, ran in circles for a few seconds, and then disappeared over the top of the ridge.

That hunt took place on the plains of eastern Montana, on the edge of huge Fort Peck Reservoir. It held most of the essential elements of successful pronghorn hunting, the last of the strictly open-country big game that is at all abundant in the lower United States today.

Like almost all open-country mammals, pronghorn depend greatly on their eyesight. Their eyes are huge, set far apart in their heads; at close range they occasionally remind me of huge grasshoppers. The resolution of those eyes has been compared often to that of a man with binoculars — let's just say that if you are close enough to a pronghorn to see his eyes, he can tell whether your pupils are dilated, even if you're wearing sunglasses.

The pronghorn has other adaptations that allow him to live on the open plains. His hair is hollow, like that of deer and caribou, but the air-spaces are even larger, allowing him to graze comfortably in the winter winds of the northern prairie. (He can also withstand the heat of the Baja Peninsula.) The pronghorn is also the fastest animal in the western hemisphere — only the cheetah of Africa and the blackbuck of India are perhaps as fast. Nobody has ever staged a race between the three, so we'll probably never know. The cheetah, most authorities feel, could probably catch a pronghorn with a quick burst of speed, but over longer distances the pronghorn is probably the fastest four-footed creature on earth.

14

My father grew up on the central plains of eastern Montana. One day, when he was driving between two small towns, a buck pronghorn near the highway started running beside the car, which was going about 45 miles an hour. My father accelerated to 50 — and so did the buck. Finally my father tromped the gas pedal and sped up to 60, as fast as he dared go on that narrow 1940 Montana highway. The buck kept pace for a short distance and then turned on the afterburner, zipping across the road in front of the car. My father claimed the buck was laughing, too, but I believe the rest of the tale. Everyone who's driven the back roads in pronghorn country for any length of time has similar stories to tell.

Even more amazing is the fact that the pronghorn can travel at 30 to 40 miles an hour for several miles. He has an oversized heart and lungs that allow him to outdistance any other prairie animal. Coyotes occasionally catch a pronghorn by running it in relays, but even a month-old antelope fawn can outrun any coyote alive.

Some observers feel that the bigger, heavier bucks are slower than the more graceful does, because the bucks always seem to bring up the rear of a running band. But bucks are never left behind by the rest of the band; for some reason they just like to run back there, perhaps as a defense measure. Buck deer and bull elk commonly behave the same way.

It is the speed and eyesight of the pronghorn that are his two greatest defense mechanisms, and the two most common hunting methods used on "prairie goats" are designed to overcome one or the other strength. Unfortunately, the method used to overcome the pronghorn's speed — chasing him with a vehicle — is not only unsporting but results in wounded animals and unsavory meat. It is, however, still common (albeit illegal) across the West.

These same people usually have contempt for pronghorn meat, and it's easy to see why after trying to choke down a steak that's been run for two or three miles. Pronghorn have large, efficient adrenal glands that kick into overdrive when the animals are alarmed, and in a matter of a few hundred yards the flesh of the animal is permeated with adrenalin, not to mention overheated. If you add to this the hot weather that may occur in early October (the most common period for pronghorn season in the West), you're likely to end up with chops tasting like the smell of a wet

15

billy goat. If you've never smelled a wet billy goat ... well, you're lucky, and that applies equally to rank pronghorn meat.

The "hunters" that chase pronghorn in pickups remind me of a bassett hound I once was acquainted with. He belonged to a rancher I worked for in southeastern Montana, and when we'd drive around the ranch, the bassett would ride along. Whenever he'd see a pronghorn, he'd go crazy — run after it, howling, his stumpy legs a reasonable facsimile of a blur. The pronghorn would saunter off at ¼-throttle, looking back now and then at this insane apparition. That dog never caught a pronghorn, but if he had, I'm sure he wouldn't have known what in the hell to do with it. People who chase pronghorns in pickups are very similar. They chase them down, shoot them, and don't know why.

A better way of hunting pronghorn is to try to sneak around their amazing eyesight. This can be done by driving to ridgetops and scanning the hills. On sunny days pronghorns can be seen for miles, even with the naked eye, because their light color contrasts with the prairie. On overcast days they're harder to spot, and good binoculars make the difference. If you're after a trophy buck, a spotting scope of 20-power or so can be helpful for evaluating horns.

After pronghorn have been located, you try to figure out how to get closer. Even though pronghorn country is usually not hilly, there are always a few dry gullies and coulees, reasonable cover for getting close to a band. Tall sagebrush helps, and is effective in obscuring the last few yards of a ridgetop. Sometimes it's so tall you can't take advantage of a solid prone shooting position, but a rifle rested on a tall specimen of sage is almost as steady.

In heavily hunted pronghorn country, though, it is sometimes hard to complete a stalk because of pickup hunters. It's easy to find murderous intent in your mind after you've walked a hot mile, crawled 100 yards through prickly pear and yucca, started to ease up behind an ideal sagebrush patch for the shot, when a pickup load of yahoos comes blasting over the hill to chase your carefully-located pronghorn into the next state.

It seems that every year it gets more difficult to find a place where you can stalk a pronghorn unmolested, but it's possible. Public hunting areas, like the huge tracts of Bureau of Land Management land that cover large parts of the sagebrush West, are most heavily hunted by pickup, so if you can find a private spread where the owner is particular about who hunts and how, you can stalk pronghorn in peace. Such spreads, however, are not easy to find, for several reasons. One is that ranchers in recent years have been hard-pressed to make ends meet, and many still believe that pronghorns gobble up valuable cattle grass (they don't — they primarily eat the forbs that grow between clumps of range grass) so they allow as much pronghorn hunting as they can, and they aren't particular about how the hunting's done. Also, ranchers are becoming aware that sportsmen are willing to pay for the privilege of hunting on private property. So if you hunt private land, you may have to pay heavily or share your privilege with a crowd of pickup hunters. Just hunting private land is becoming less of a guarantee of good pronghorn hunting.

Some hunters take advantage of pronghorn chasers and sit in one place, hoping that a herd of antelope will pass by. On hard-hunted tracts this can work well; good spots to watch are low saddles between ridges, and waterholes. Pronghorn that are getting chivvied around naturally get thirsty, and are apt to visit watering spots more often than they normally do. Just find a relatively concealed spot a couple of hundred yards downwind of a saddle or waterhole and you're in business. Winds are usually strong and steady on the prairie, and you should consider them when planning a stalk or a sitting place, but pronghorn aren't as dependent on their noses as game animals from more vegetated country, so the wind isn't quite so critical.

I prefer to hunt my pronghorns where no one else is around; one of the best ways to do that on public land is to use a method of transportation that most other hunters don't. That pronghorn hunt on Fort Peck Reservoir is a good example — the piece of country we boated to is roadless, and you rarely find pronghorn hunters more than a mile or so from their vehicle. There are a surprising number of places on the "dry" plains where you can stalk a prairie goat by boat, most of them provided by the Army Corps of Engineers or the Bureau of Reclamation (not everything the two agencies do is a total disaster). Fort Peck is a 150-mile-long lake that cuts right through the heart of Montana's pronghorn range. Similar reservoirs, such as Oahe and Sakakawea, cover hundreds of miles of prime pronghorn territory in the Dakotas; and Glendo, Pathfinder, Seminoe, Fontenelle and Flaming Gorge do the same in Wyoming. An added advantage in this kind of hunting is that pronghorn live in dry country, and if given a choice, they like to stay close to water. I don't think I've ever been to Fort Peck, Flaming Gorge, or Oahe without spotting at least a few pronghorn on the shore. Such vast reservoirs are usually accesssible at only a few points (there are eight official access points along the 1500-odd miles of Fort Peck's shoreline, for instance), leaving a lot of places where pronghorns can loll about close to their beloved H_2O.

Horses are also practical hunting "vehicles" over much of the West. Hard-hunted pronghorn tend to drift into two types of areas: flat spaces so wide that hunters can't get within rifle range without being seen, or country more rugged than most hunters are willing to travel. It's this second kind of terrain that is especially adaptable to hunting by horse. When I worked on that ranch in southwestern Montana I often had to ride the 15,000 acres, shifting cattle from pasture to pasture, or rounding up recalcitrant bulls, and it was startling how often I'd jump big pronghorn bucks from rugged badlands coulees. In fact, the biggest buck I've ever seen alive I almost ran over one time when I was out looking for a lost bull. His horns were in the 16 to 17 inch class, an enormous buck. He didn't get that big by allowing hunters to get close to him, and I believe the only reason I got so close was that I was riding a horse. Pronghorn on livestock ranges are used to the sounds of cattle and horses, and often mingle with grazing livestock, something that deer rarely do.

Of course, rough country is equally accessible to foot hunters, but a horse is not only an easier way of getting around and familiar to the pronghorn, but handy for getting a carcass out of the hills. Pronghorn are not large beasts — a mature buck I weighed a few years ago only went 85 pounds field-dressed, and a Nebraska survey found very few bucks over 90 — and a good horse can easily handle one tied behind the saddle, as well as the rider.

An odd thing I noticed while riding is that pronghorn eyesight isn't nearly as effective at short ranges. Apparently they're used to gazing out over the prairie at distances of hundreds of yards, and a horse and rider suddenly coming on them at perhaps 50 yards confuses them. I particularly remember one buck I startled while I was mending fence. He was nibbling shrubs in the bottom of a 30-foot-deep coulee, and when I suddenly appeared at the top,

18

he jumped straight up like a cartoon cat, then trotted stiff-legged up the other side of the coulee. He was a fairly large buck, with horns in the 13-14-inch class, so he'd obviously been around for a few years, but he stood on the hillside, not 50 yards away, peering at me, every few moments giving a startled "chuff!" — a sort of half-coughing, half-blowing sound that startled prong-horns emit. Evidently he just couldn't figure out what sort of beast I was, and he was still standing there trying to figure it out when I rode away.

Pronghorn are inquisitive animals, and Indians and early plains hunters used to "flag" them — put a bandana or a piece of white leather on a stick and wave it back and forth to attract curious pronghorns into range of bows or blackpowder rifles. It still works occasionally, but I've never used it while hunting, simply be-cause it rarely attracts pronghorn older than yearlings. I have flagged pronghorn during photo sessions, but any animal more than a year or two old won't come closer, though often they'll stand and stare instead of trotting off. Once I was trying to take a photo of a young buck near Circle, Montana. He was several hundred yards out in a field near a highway, and I was trying to get him to come closer to my 400mm telephoto lens. I stood behind a fencepost, waving my arms, sticking my legs out, hoot-ing like an owl. I didn't get the pronghorn to come any closer but I attracted a lot of tourists passing by on the highway. That buck would just stand and "chuff!" and stamp his feet, but he wouldn't come nearer. After a few gunshots have sounded on opening day, pronghorn become even shyer.

In fact, early morning on opening day is about the only time you might be able to flag up a young pronghorn. Actually, in most areas, you don't hunt on opening morning — you hunt the days before. As I've noted, undisturbed pronghorn don't move around much — if you can locate a good band a day or two before the opener, they'll be somewhere nearby at dawn of the first day of the season. Don't be discouraged if they happen to see you when you're scouting, either. A few years ago I was out looking for pronghorn in northeastern Montana, and through a bit of sloppy work managed to startle a buck and doe out of a little basin back in some badlands. They tore off over the hill like they'd just read about a sagebrush sale in the next county. I didn't go near the area again until opening day, and at daybreak found the buck back in

19

that basin. I don't know where his girlfriend was, but I wasn't after her. He ended up in my freezer. I do know, however, that if he'd been shot at, he wouldn't have returned, and that if he'd heard the distant shots of opening day, he'd have been more alert, and I might not have been able to sneak up on him.

If you don't manage to get a pronghorn on opening day, hunting gets progressively worse for about a week. Pronghorn get wilder and wilder as they're chased around, shot at, and otherwise disturbed. If you're after any pronghorn, it is still possible to harvest a doe or young buck during this period, but if you're after a good buck, it's perhaps better to wait until the tumult and shouting have died and hunt the last part of the season. Pronghorn season in most states starts well before deer season, and there's often a gap of a week or two after opening week of the pronghorn season and the deer opener. This is usually a good time to look for a trophy, as the pickup hunters will have had their one-day thrill and no deer hunters will be out. Mid-week periods are good, too, as casual hunters tend to be weekenders. Even the tag end of the season can be good, but there is the possibility of snow, which makes pronghorn hard to spot, even with binoculars.

Good pronghorn country is typified by lots of sagebrush, for two reasons. One is that sagebrush is an open-country food source that remains available during a hard winter. Open grasslands are fine pronghorn range during summer and fall, but a good layer of wind-crusted snow causes difficulty for pronghorn, which don't have the strength to continually dig through snow for food. Sagebrush, especially the larger varieties, sticks well above the snowline, unless the winter is unusually severe, and provides a surprisingly good diet, being relatively high in protein.

The second reason that sagebrush country is good pronghorn country is that it's wide-open, with few fences. Pronghorn feel secure where they can see for long distances, and they're not crazy about fences. Although prongrhorn can make tremendous bounds horizontally, they don't like to jump vertically, like deer; but in a few areas, they've learned to jump fences, where fencing is common. Where fences aren't common, pronghorn prefer to go under instead of over, which is relatively easy with the standard 3 or 4-wire barbed cattle fence. "Sheep" fences, however, which are of woven wire to keep small stock from getting through, can cause problems. Sheep fences are used along inter-state highway right-of-ways; while driving in southern Wyoming I once encountered a mature pronghorn buck that had somehow wandered onto the freeway. He was almost totally exhausted, desperately looking for a way off the right-of-way and back onto the open range. Every time a car passed he tried to dash under the woven fence, but couldn't. He never even tried to jump the 4-foot barrier. He eventually came to a cattle guard and hopped across it, but by that time he looked as though he'd had a bad Saturday night.

Some hunters claim that pronghorn that eat sagebrush taste sagey, and so only hunt in grassy areas, but those hunters are usually pickup-chasing types, and I've noticed that a large number of their "grassland" pronghorn taste bad — a phenome-non those hunters attribute to pronghorn "just coming from" sage country. The best pronghorn I've ever eaten came from sage range. The key to good pronghorn meat is a quick kill, a clean job of field-dressing (scrupulously avoid getting the brittle hair on the meat — this imparts a bitter taste), and, in warm weather, getting the hide off the animal as quickly as possible. Pronghorn are small beasts, and even a big buck will cool down quickly if skinned and hung in a shady place or, if possible, in a cool meat locker; and splitting the carcass along the backbone with a meat saw will help in warm weather. Good pronghorn meat is among the best big game, having a mild, slightly sweet taste. Many people who claim to dislike venison go wild over properly-cared-for pronghorn. Pronghorn liver is also mild; I never liked liver until I tasted that of a doe pronghorn I shot several years ago. It has almost none of the "strong" taste of beef or pork liver. The liver and heart should be rinsed in cool water as soon as possible after the kill; I take a jug of water along on pronghorn hunts for just that purpose, and also to rinse out the body cavity, especially if any hair has chanced to fall into it. Excessive water, however, can promote spoilage, but if you wipe the body cavity as much as possible with paper towels, the warm weather of most pronghorn country will quickly dry the rest, and you'll have meat that anyone will love to eat.

Does are perhaps better eating than big bucks, but a buck properly cared for is acceptable, so if you're interested in trophy hunting don't assume that the meat will be inedible. Take good care of it.

What constitutes a trophy pronghorn? In some hard-hunted areas, any buck can be a trophy, but for most purposes mature bucks with horns over a foot long around the curve are considered fair trophies. Anything over 14 inches is considered worth the expense and trouble of a taxidermist, and anything over 16 a tremendous trophy. Probably only a small fraction of the 1% of pronghorn harvested every year have horns that long, and all are candidates for the record book.

Judging trophies is a skill that is acquired slowly and through experience. A basic rule of thumb is based on the length of a pronghorn's ears. If the horns are twice as long as the ears, the animal is probably a mature buck of 12-13 inches; much longer than that and you are looking at a fine trophy. If you're interested in a large trophy buck but have little hunting experience, hiring a good guide makes sense. An experienced pronghorn man can judge horns to within a half-inch or even closer, from hundreds of yards away (using binoculars and spotting scope). If that extra inch or half-inch means a lot to you, I'd certainly advise hiring a guide.

I personally have little interest in getting a buck that will "make the book" though I am by no means only a meat hunter. The total experience of the hunt is far more important to me than an extra inch of horn, and whether or not my name will appear in the records is far from my mind. A nice set of horns of a Montana buck are on the wall above me as I write this, but they are not anywhere near record size. Just under 13 inches long when fresh, they have heavy, wide bases. But those are statistics, and like many statistics, they are interesting but irrelevant. The horns are on my wall not because of their size, but because they remind me of a stalk I once made along a sandy beach, and of all the instants that made up that hunting memory. For me, all of that hunt was a "trophy", the reason those horns are on my wall.

Where To Go

Wyoming is and always has been the top pronghorn state, with the annual harvest running around 40,000 animals, about a tenth of the total pronghorn population on this continent. Habitat is the reason. Pronghorn need sagebrush, and Wyoming is to sagebrush

22

as Milwaukee is to beer. The northeastern section, the middle part of the Green River Valley, and the area around Rawlins are probably the best areas; about the only place you won't find pronghorn in Wyoming is the northwestern corner of the state, where there just aren't many sagebrush valleys.

Montana is a consistent second to Wyoming as a pronghorn state, with the annual kill running about half of Wyoming's. The best areas are the south-central part and the area around Fort Peck Reservoir.

Elsewhere the pickings get increasingly slim, with North and South Dakota probably the best areas. Pronghorn are found in the western parts of both states, and in the northwestern and north-central portions of Nebraska, but amount to only a small fraction of the Wyoming-Montana herds. Eastern Colorado is good but crowded.

Texas offers pronghorn hunting in the Panhandle, and New Mexico in the northeastern corner, but the New Mexico hunting is very limited. A few pronghorn are also found in Kansas, Oklahoma, Utah, Idaho, Oregon and southern Canada, but these areas are not the best, awarding few permits or restricting hunting to residents only.

Mule deer are the largest of the commonly-hunted plains big game. This specimen weighed over 240 pounds dressed.

Chapter Three: Mule Deer

Odocoileus hemionus

There was nothing over there but an open slope, but somehow we knew something was wrong. Perhaps hunters develop a sense that tells them when game is near — but it was more likely that we had noticed a shadow. Ben saw the deer first, as one of its big ears flicked, and then it was running, antlers widespread past those big ears, around the point of the ridge. We each took a quick shot that did nothing but throw rocks and dirt on the buck's rear end.

That big mule deer had been sitting almost in plain sight, behind a thin fringe of scraggly sagebrush, but even from the opposite hillside, a short 150 yards away, we hadn't been able to see him until he moved. What we had seen, what had kept us looking at that apparently empty Montana slope, was the shadow of his head. Somehow it hadn't seemed right that a shadow should fall across the grama grass without something to make it.

Mule deer are the original open-country deer. They'll sit out in sparse, open cover, brush that barely breaks up their outlines, brush that would make the average whitetail feel like an ungulate Lady Godiva. Mule deer aren't as shy as whitetail, either, and many western hunters consider them "dumb." Every plains hunter has tales of mule deer stopping on the ridge for one last

25

shot, or simply standing still and looking at the hunter from short range. One common piece of advice when I was learning to hunt deer as a Montana teenager was to shout or whistle when you jumped a mule deer — supposedly they'd stop and look back. Sometimes it worked, too.

Similar experiences still happen. Three years ago a companion and I stood on a badlands promontory in eastern Montana and watched two "hunters" fire a total of 14 shots at a forkhorn muley buck they'd jumped from a sage-lined coulee below. They had semi-automatic rifles and spare loaded clips. The deer was only 60 or 70 yards off when they jumped it and started bounding in that peculiar stiff-legged mule deer bounce over the sage. Each of the hunters emptied one clip trying to intercept that bounce. They were in the middle of their second clip when the little buck stopped at the head of a draw a couple of hundred yards away and looked back, standing broadside, to see what had spooked him. One of the hunters calmed down, sat down, and shot him.

Young bucks and does will still behave this way, but over most of the West, the mule deer has become harder to collect over the past 10 or 20 years, partly because there aren't as many of them — the huge mule deer populations of the '50's and early '60's are gone now, the result of too many deer then and too many people now. But mule deer are also harder to collect because the easy deer were killed off, and natural selection has produced the progeny of deer that didn't stop and look back.

The plains mule deer had an even harder time of it than his mountain cousin. The intensification of agriculture since World War II has not helped the mule deer, who can't get along well when his habitat is bounded by wheatfields or overgrazed by cattle. At one time, mule deer were found almost to the eastern limits of the grasslands, into Iowa and Minnesota. While a few mule deer are occasionally seen in Minnesota, they're not common even in the eastern portions of any mid-prairie states like the Dakotas and Nebraska. Good plains mule deer hunting has its eastern limits on the farthest western edge of the grasslands; a line drawn from the western third of North Dakota down through the Oklahoma and Texas Panhandles would just about delineate the best open-country muley area.

Though I've found mule deer in the same sort of cottonwood-willow riverbottom cover as whitetail, where their ranges over-

26

lap, mule deer prefer country that is more up-and-down than whitetail habitat. Not only does it suit their temperament better — as I noted, they're fond of sitting on almost open hillsides, where they can have a view — but such areas are usually less bothered by man.

There's one coulee in a jumble of rugged breaks in eastern Montana that I've hunted on and off for six or eight years. I've only seen three deer there, but all were mule deer, and that coulee lies in an area that is almost totally dominated by whitetails. That place is known to some local hunters as "Blacktail Coulee" — "blacktail" being a common colloquialism for mule deer over much of the West — because it is one of the few spots in that flat region where mule deer can be found. Similarly, most of North Dakota is whitetail country, except for the southwestern part, the region that holds the famous Badlands. Both kinds of deer are found in that corner of the state, but the whitetails are almost all down in the riverbottoms; they leave the rugged breaks and gumbo buttes to the mule deer. On a photographic expedition in Theodore Roosevelt National Memorial Park one fall, I was trying to stalk some bighorn sheep with a telephoto lens, in some of the biggest, most rugged badlands I've ever seen. The red sides of those hills were about as straight up-and-down as any non-rock hills can be — and right in the middle of my stalk I jumped a three-point mule deer buck out of a patch of chokecherry near the top of one of the rugged buttes.

Since mule deer are usually found in sparser cover than whitetails, a common method for hunting them on the plains is to use binoculars to spot them from a distance, then to make a stalk. This is more difficult than it sounds because mule deer, unlike pronghorns, blend remarkably well with the tan-gray of autumn hills. Their coats at that time of year are almost gray, and even deer standing out in the open are difficult to see. To someone unpracticed in looking for them they can be invisible. When I was in high school, I was hunting with a friend who'd never hunted deer before. We came over a ridge one morning, and on the opposite slope, 200 yards away, were about 20 mule deer, standing and feeding slowly in the morning sun. For the next 15 minutes I tried to explain where the deer were.

"Look, you see that two-trunked ponderosa? Look about 30 feet below it and a little left...

"There's a big gray rock. A buck is standing just to the right of it..."

When he finally did shoot, he shot that rock.

Experienced deer hunters, whether whitetail experts or mule deer sages, will tell you they look for part of a deer. That's an easy concept to understand when you're talking about stalking a deer in thick cover — 99% of the time most of a deer will be covered by branches. But it also applies to spotting mule deer in open country. Part of my friend's problem was that he was looking for a deer's body, and a gray mule deer against a gray hillside is an inconspicuous item, especially in overcast or flat light. Instead he should have looked for smaller pieces of the deer. A mule deer's ears, for instance, are often lighter than the rest of the animal, and stick out like a big V against a hillside. They're moving much of the time, too, flicking in little movements that are easy to spot once you know what to look for. The other end of a mule deer, too, is conspicuous: anytime you see a white circle bisected by a black-tipped line you know you're looking at a mule deer rear. Shadows help, like the one the big buck at the beginning of this chapter threw. I've occasionally spotted a shadow floating on a hillside when there wasn't any apparent reason for it, and looked upward to find a mule deer on top of the shadow.

The best times for glassing are morning and evening, as the deer are more apt to be moving then, and it's always easier to spot moving deer than bedded ones. Clear days are best, too, because you may catch a slight glint off an antler, and shadows are more prominent. Overcast days flatten everything out.

Another popular method for mule deer hunting on the plains is coulee walking. Usually two hunters will walk either side of a brushy draw. Mule deer are much more easily driven from cover then whitetails and will usually leave brush without much coax- ing. If you're after a young deer and don't care about trophies, this is an excellent method, as the younger deer will commonly stop for that last — very last — muley look. Big bucks, however, just don't do that anymore, and a running mule deer, because of its jackrabbit bounce, is a difficult moving target. Watching a hunter aiming at a bouncing muley is like watching the crowd at a tennis match — except the hunter's movement is up-and-down, not side-to-side.

Truly large mule deer bucks are perhaps the greatest big game challenge an open-country hunter can find. Big bucks prefer the most rugged places, the really snarling stretches of badlands and breaks. Big deer pose many problems, not the least of which is getting the carcass out. Occasionally you can drive the ridge-tops in badlands, and this is a common method in some areas. Badlands, geologically, are usually places that used to be flat, where erosion has scoured away the topsoil. In the "newer" pieces of badlands, long "fingers" of sod may stretch out into rugged country, offering routes for wheeled hunters. Unfortunately, greater access also pushes the big bucks farther back into broken country, and you probably will end up walking anyway after you get to the end of four-wheel-drive trails.

Many times I've casually sat on a relatively open hillside and glassed a slope for smaller mule deer, but the hunter who tries such tactics on big bucks will end up with no meat in the freezer and no antlers on the wall. Big mule deer bucks need three basic things: a vantage point where they can rest unmolested (usually with at least two escape routes) and water and food close by. Rough country bucks will often choose as their resting spot a patch of juniper or other small trees on the ridge point between two big coulees, and they are difficult to approach in such a spot. They're also nervous about being seen; younger deer may sit and look back at a hunter glassing them from the opposite slope, but big bucks are up and gone the moment they're sure they've been spotted.

The one advantage for a hunter who's seen a big buck in his hiding spot is that the buck will be reluctant to give his spot up. Open-country mule deer, in my experience, are more reluctant to travel long distances to water than whitetail, though there are exceptions. A big muley who's found a backcountry stock dam or spring with a nice vantage point near isn't about to give it up — at least as long as he hasn't been shot at. If you do happen to roust a buck from his hideout, don't shoot at him unless the chance is reasonably sure, and in a day or two approach the spot more circumspectly. A dry year will often produce good hunting because the deer are more reluctant to leave the few watering spots available.

Boat-hunting for bigger mule deer is an excellent tactic in some western areas — especially in the breaks that have been partially flooded by the numerous reservoirs created by the magical Corps of Engineers across the western plains. One big advantage to hunting breaks and badlands by boat is that if you do shoot a deer, getting him to the boat involves downhill work, instead of the uphill haul that normally results from hunting from wheeled vehicles.

The semi-open ponderosa pine forests that top some of the higher breaks of the northern plains also offer good mule deer hunting. This is almost timber hunting, but the country consists, usually, of pine-topped ridges over open slopes. The standard tactic is to stalk carefully through the pines, glassing the opposite slopes, during morning and evening, and possibly working the thicker timber during the middle of the day. Rarely does snowfall have as big an impact on the hunting in these hills as it does in the mountains farther west, because the really heavy plains snowfalls usually occur after hunting season has ended, so mid-day hunting is noisy and tough. Hunting carefully around the few water sources during the mid-day period can pay off, however.

Mule deer can also be found out on the sage flats. The normal way to hunt the flats is to rest your rear just below a ridge and carefully scan the country with binoculars, especially early and late in the day. Mule deer will also have definite routes they travel in sage country, though on a vastly larger scale than the trails made by breaks deer, because they must travel farther to water. I was hunting near Fort Peck Reservoir in Montana one November day and had just about given up — legal light was almost gone and I was thirsty, walking back toward my pickup, parked half-a-mile away. I'd just walked around the edge of the only tract of gumbo buttes that could be seen within miles when a dozen doe mule deer trotted around the edge of one of the buttes. It was getting late in the season, so I sat down and broke one's neck with my .270. It wasn't until I'd dressed the doe and started dragging it toward my pickup that I noticed the area seemed to be covered with deer trails that twisted between the tall sagebrush. Evidently the deer traveled along the side of that butte on their way to a small stock dam half-a-mile away for their evening drink. I had to wait another year to prove my theory, but another November day found me ensconced on the side of the butte. About 15 minutes before sundown two bucks came by, one a three-pointer and one a middling four-pointer. They were about 150 yards away, and when they paused to sniff the air, my hunt ended.

30

Sagebrush deer "routes" can cover long distances, at least in comparison to trails in other areas, and can cover a broad area, perhaps 100 or 200 yards across. They are routes, however, albeit less traveled than those used by deer in breaks or forests. Usually they skirt the edges of definite geographic features, such as a butte, or follow the coulees, and are usually traversed more during the evening than the morning, at least in my observations. Again I've found that the really big bucks travel different — and shorter — routes than does and young bucks, so just watching any sagebrush trail doesn't mean you'll see a big buck. For that, try the roughest piece of country you can find.

Where to Go

Montana and Wyoming offer the very best open-country mule deer hunting. Montana's best areas are the Custer National Forest sections in the southwestern part of the state and the Missouri Breaks in the central portion. Northeastern Wyoming's sage valleys have good-sized mule deer, with muleys being found generally throughout the eastern valleys.

Mule deer are scarce but huntable in the southern plains portions of Alberta and Saskatchewan (with Saskatchewan hunting limited to Canadians). North Dakota's best mule deer area is around the Badlands area in the southwest. South Dakota's deer are almost all found west of the Missouri River in the more-rugged breaks, especially in the southern area.

Eastern Colorado and western Kansas have a few open-country mule deer. Colorado's are mostly confined to the northeastern section, and Kansas' deer to the northwest. The Kansas mule deer seasons are usually for residents only.

Oklahoma's mule deer population seems to be rising in portions of the Panhandle and extreme northwest, especially in Cimarron County. There's also good hunting to be found in parts of the Texas Panhandle, especially in the northwestern corner.

Open-country mule deer can also be found throughout the drier valleys of the rest of the West, especially Nevada and Utah, but this is really more desert than true plains country.

Chapter Four:
Other Big Game

(Buffalo, bighorn sheep, and elk)

If you suddenly developed a yearning to hunt buffalo (bison, to purists) you could easily do so provided you had about 500 spare bucks and a big enough freezer. How? There are several "buffalo ranches" in the West where the sportsman after a head mount, black robe, and 1000 pounds of carcass can shoot the buffalo of his choice for about that price. Some ranches have graduated scales, depending on the size beast you want. In most cases you pay your money, drive around the ranch until you spot the specimen you want, lean over the hood and shoot him; then comes the most difficult part of the "hunt", arranging what's to be done with the carcass. The whole process is not hunting in the strict sense, but it's the most practical method of getting a buffalo today. There is one area in Utah, the Henry Mountains, where the wild buffalo roam (and the deer and the antelope play) and hunting is permitted. There are very few permits sold each year, each hotly sought for by several thousand aspiring Buffalo Bills. It is not plains hunting, but from what I have heard, it is really hunting, and the animals are not penned up and semi-tame. The big problem may be getting the damn beast out of the mountains once it's shot. Why, hell, I've spent a couple of days getting an elk only a mile to the nearest road. What do you do with a two-elk-sized buffalo ten miles from nowhere?

32

There are two schools of thought concerning buffalo rifles. (I mean, there are some people that still consider that question.) One is to use a big gun for the big game. The other is to use a small gun and shoot the buffalo in the ear, not at all impossible on many ranches. I'll leave this argument up to those who desire to shoot such an animal. If you have a spare .50-110 Sharps lying around, it might be appropriate.

A few badlands bighorns are also available. Both Montana and North Dakota have planted bighorns in some badlands country. Montana gives out two rare and priceless ram permits a year for the area south of Miles City, in the southeastern part of the state, and North Dakota has allowed hunts for state residents only. I would love to try one of these hunts, but I doubt that I'll ever shoot a badlands bighorn with anything except a telephoto lens.

Elk are also available through special permits. Montana has a few areas along Fort Peck Reservoir where elk are harvested; but these elk are also accessible to any bowhunter, without going through a drawing. A word of warning, though — every eastern Montana bowhunter and his North Dakota buddy will be scrambling through the breaks after the few wapiti there.

Saskatchewan has some elk, but they are mainly limited to the forests of the northern part of the province, and hunting them doesn't qualify as a plains elk hunt. In addition, they're not available to non-Canadians.

Oklahoma, surprisingly, has a few elk, confined to refuge areas in the east and southwest. These are also only huntable through special permits.

Both Montana and Oklahoma open-country elk are not in strictly open country, but in patches of semi-open forest (the type of habitat Lewis and Clark hunted them in along the midwestern Missouri), so long-range guns aren't usually necessary.

Wooly mammoths and saber-toothed tigers are just about gone on the plains except for a few living in a trailer park outside of Sandbar, Nebraska. Nobody bothers them much.

Chapter Five:
Plains Rifles and Bows

The Basics

A hunter about to make his first plains big game trip after mule deer or pronghorn often forsakes the trusty .308 he's been using to harvest whitetails in Pennsylvania. In a fever of anticipation, he's read every article he can find on shooting in the Wide-Open Spaces and the rifles used out there. Many of those articles say that since the West is big and the men out there strong, the rifles used must also be big and tough. Our friend is convinced that a 7mm Magnum, or maybe even a .300, is needed to make those "cross-canyon" shots on big mule deer, or to reach a pronghorn that's posing a quarter of a mile away across a sage flat. So he cashes in the kids' college bonds and makes the local hardware store owner happy by laying down several hundred hard green bills for a shiny Magnum with a big variable scope. Maybe he even buys a box of shells and shoots the thing once or twice before he hops in the family Ford and wends his way to Wyoming.

At the other extreme is the natural-born firearms wizard who's killed every deer in his life with the same old iron-sighted .303

British jungle carbine he bought for 15 bucks back in high school. Why, just last fall he killed the biggest buck taken in the whole county with one Remington 215-grain load. Hit him right in the middle of the left ventricle, too. This guy can't see any reason to buy a new rifle just because he's going after pronghorn in Montana. He'll just hold a little higher is all, to allow for the drop of that semi-somnolent bullet.

Each of these experienced hunters is off base, of course. One is expecting his equipment to do the job for him, and the other is expecting his past experience to totally overcome a totally different set of shooting conditions.

How close are these fictional shooters to reality? Surprisingly close — in fact, they're all too real. Among my hunting companions is a rancher who runs cattle over about 20 square miles of southeastern Montana's mule deer and pronghorn territory. Each fall he takes a little time off from chasing cows to ferry a few Eastern hunters around his place, trying to get them a shot at one or the other of those two big game animals. And every fall he has several new stories to tell about how this dude and that dude couldn't hit one of his Hereford bulls in the butt with buckshot. He just can't figure out why these men will spend a year's savings to come out West for a big hunt and will not bring the proper equipment or practice for the hunt. A couple of years ago he finally nailed together a crude benchrest out by the haystacks, and now he makes every hunter sit down at that bench and prove he can hit a paper plate at 50 paces.

And, yes, a lot of them can't do it.

He also gets more insistent every year that hunters show up that will reach a pronghorn at 250 yards. He's had scads of hunters bring iron-sighted .30-30's — one character even showed up with a .44 Magnum carbine, bragging on all the one-shot whitetail kills he'd made back in Vermont. My rancher friend is also prejudiced against the .30-06 — which is actually a good plains caliber — because so many of his guidees show up with '06 ammo loaded with roundnosed 180- or 220-grain bullets. Such loads, as he so colorfully explains, "bloop real bad" — meaning they have a trajectory like a meekly-struck softball. He doesn't like the .308, either, or "them damn automatics." Now, just what is a good open-country rifle? Let's look at the shooting requirements. In spite of the fact that pronghorn and even mule

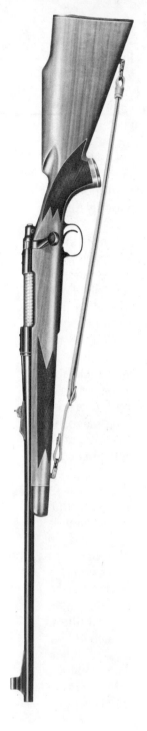

REMINGTON ARMS CO.

Most experienced plains hunters prefer bolt-action rifles because of their accuracy. Left-handed bolt-actioned guns are available from several manufacturers, bringing the advantages of this type of arm to southpaw shooters.

BROWNING ARMS CO.

Falling block single shot rifles make elegant and practical rifles for open-country hunting. Available in modern calibers and equipped with good scope sights, they are especially suitable for pronghorn hunting.

36

deer are occasionally taken at ranges beyond 300 yards, the average shot is not that far. Most mule deer are taken at under 200, and prairie whitetails even closer. Not that long shots don't turn up now and then — but most of the time, the mule deer you spot from a quarter of a mile away is easily approached to a saner range. People who constantly bubble about the long shots they make (or attempt) either don't know enough to stalk a big game animal or are too lazy to try.

What we need, then, is a firearm able to take game consistently up to 250 yards, with enough power to punch through the shoulder blade of a big deer. It must also be reasonably quick-handling, as many Western deer are taken, after being jumped from brush, at ranges of 50-150 yards. Even a young mule deer that stands and looks at the hunter isn't going to make like the Statue of Liberty all day, and the quicker a sure shot is made the better.

Those are broad requirements, but you'll find a broad array of firearms suitable for open-country hunting. Many of the rifles my rancher friend curses as "bloopers" are entirely suitable for plains hunting — it's not the firearms themselves that are unfit but the way in which they're used. In fact, the "brush carbine" you use on whitetails may be nearly as good as that rancher's .270, if used correctly, and used improperly, the very .270 he touts may become a poor open-country gun.

The biggest failing of my friend's clients is an almost practiced ignorance of their guns' capabilities. Some show up at the ranch door assuming that any centerfire rifle will "shoot flat" for a mile or more. Others are also convinced that you must "hold over" for 250 yards when shooting with a .30-06. Some don't have the foggiest notion where to hold and couldn't care less.

The first idea to divest yourself of is that any rifle "shoots flat." The path of a bullet is curved, and all bullets start falling the instant they leave the muzzle. A "flat-shooting" rifle, like a .270, just has a less-curved trajectory. If you have a .30-06, for instance, and are using the 180-grain roundnosed bullet at about 2700 feet per second (fps) muzzle velocity, and if you have the rifle sighted in so that the bullets strike the center of a bullseye at 100 yards, your shot will hit about 20" below your point of aim at 300 yards, out where your trophy pronghorn is dancing in the sun. A .270, however, using a 130-grain spitzer (pointed) bullet at about 3100 fps and using the same sight-in, will strike about 11″ low at 300 yards. The .280 shoots about twice as "flat" as the '06.

Actually neither gun is properly set up for that 300-yard shot. Even the 11″ drop of the .270 bullet would miss the chest of a big deer if the hunter were aiming for the center of the deer's chest. The very largest deer are no more than a foot-and-a-half deep through the chest. A mid-chest aim would result in the bullet's striking 2″ below the bottom of the deer's ribs, hardly conducive to successful hunting.

There is, however, a way to make sure that the .270 will strike the deer squarely in the chest. Merely sighting-in the rifle so that the bullet strikes a little high at 100 yards will raise the 300-yard impact considerably. A 1½″ raising at 100 yards, for instance, will bring the point of impact at 300 yards up a full 5½″! The bullet will then strike only 6½″ low. A mid-chest hold on a big deer with a rifle sighted in this way will have the bullet landing in the lower chest, assuming a perfect shot by the hunter. Even better is to sight the .270 3″ high at 100 yards; it then strikes only about 2″ low at 300. True, it will be about 4″ above the point of aim at 200 yards, but 4″ on the side of a deer makes little difference. The main point is that our .270-equipped hunter is now able to sight on the middle of a deer's chest all the way out to 300 yards, and kill the deer.

Let's see what happens with our poor .30-06 man. With a mere flick of the pocketbook (for a box of 150-grain spitzer loads, starting at about 2900 fps) and a few clicks on the scope adjustment, we have his old "blooper" shooting 3″ high at 100 yards and only about 5″ low at 300. Even a .308 "brush gun" with a short barrel will give a 150-grain bullet about 2700 fps — sighted 3″ high at 100 yards this bullet will strike about 2″ low at 250 yards. Ah, yes, any pronghorn in Wyoming will now be in real danger.

This sighting system is well-known to knowledgeable open-country hunters, but many "average" hunters haven't been exposed to it. Essentially it means that for 90% of the shots you'll ever take in open-country a properly sighted-in .308 or .30-06 is fine, and that if you have a good rifle in one of those calibers that you're used to using, there's no real reason to buy a .25-06 or .270 just for that trip West. Even those two calibers will only extend the range at which you can hold "right on" a big game animal's chest about 50 yards over the range of a .308.

Perhaps a requirement more important than a flat trajectory is accuracy. Even if you buy the hottest magnum around, it won't work worth a damn for even 250-yard shots if you can't count on it hitting the target. Most deer hunters are satisfied if their rifle will keep most if its shots inside a 3" bullseye at 100 yards. This is roughly equivalent to a 7½" group at 250 yards, which would seem to be more than adquate even for the miniscule pronghorn, as the vital chest organs of an antelope present a target about 10" in diameter. What gives this assumption a good back-alley working over is that few of us can shoot perfectly! It's true that your bullet, *if* your hold is as immovable as Farrah Fawcett's face, *if* you squeeze the trigger like a ... well, we'll leave that fantasy up to you, *if* you are shooting on a calm day, *if* the pronghorn is frozen like one of Madame Tussaud's waxen images — well you get the point. If at least one of those conditions is not true, you have a good chance of missing or wounding the pronghorn, because that 7½" group at 250 yards leaves only 1¼" around the edges of the pronghorn's imaginary 10" vital area for error.

I'll tell you something right now — you can't shoot perfectly and neither can I. The one guy that could was John Wayne and he just lost it when he wasn't in front of a camera.

Long range magnifies the little things that can draw a shot slightly off: When the wind is blowing; when you are weary after bouncing over sagebrush all day; or when your pulse is pounding in your ear and something says you should have jogged an extra mile each day or passed up a few baked potatoes, because even prairie hills are steep.

All the accuracy you can squeeze out of a rifle will help offset these factors. A rifle that groups into an inch at 100 yards, for instance, will keep its shots inside 3" at 250, leaving about 3½" around the edges of our previously-mentioned vital area for shooter error. How much difference will that make? A lot — so much that I'll work endlessly developing handloads that are just ¼" better at 100 yards than my previous best load. That little ¼" at 100 steps makes a big difference way out there, and if you've just laid out a grand for a guided hunt in one of the best pronghorn areas in Wyoming, every little bit counts.

The shooter who buys his gun off the hardware-store rack and his ammo from the shelf below is limited in what he can do to improve his firearm's accuracy, but today's better bolt-action rifles and ammunition usually are good enough to keep all that shooter's shots inside 2" at 100 yards, which is fine if he's going to limit himself to 250-yard shooting. Many bolt-action factory rifles will group into 1-1½" with factory ammo these days, adequate for all shooting.

The dedicated gun freak and handloader can usually choke an extra bit of accuracy out of his firearm, by trying different combinations of bullet, powder, primer, and case, until he finds one that's just right for his rifle. The non-handloader can do the same by trying different brands of ammo, but since his variables are more limited he's not as likely to hit upon a combination able to knock the fleas off a coyote at 300 yards.

I've only mentioned bolt-actioned rifles up to this point, primarily because I regard them as the best tools for plains hunting. The other types of rifles — the lever-action, pump, semi-auto, and falling-block single shot — are all good firearms, and like all of today's top-of-the-line factory guns are much better than their predecessors of even 15 years ago. The reason I choose bolt-actions for all of my open-country shooting is that even though the average off-the-shelf bolt gun may not be much more accurate than any other type, it can be modified in many ways to improve its accuracy. If you have bought a lever or semi-auto that just isn't grouping the way you'd like it to, you're pretty well stuck. Almost any bolt-action rifle, though, can be made more accurate in some way by eliminating the factors that may be preventing it from reaching its potential, like reworking the bedding of the stock, adjusting the trigger, and making numerous other changes that true cross-eyed gun nuts (like me) feel compelled to make. The falling-block single shot is perhaps as accurate as the bolt, but I prefer the insurance of a quickly-available repeat shot.

When I first started hunting prairie whitetails, I often thought that a semi-auto or pump might be a better gun than a bolt. One year I chanced upon a good used pump '06 for a reasonable price. I only took one deer with it — a mid-sized whitetail buck that I missed with the first shot as he jumped from a chokecherry thicket, and killed with the second shot as he topped a ridge. Could I have made that quick second shot with a bolt-action rifle? I don't know, but I doubt it. But I soon sold the pump for several reasons, one being that I could never get groups better than about 2½" out of it, the other that the damn sliding forearm rattled like Death's chains. I also realized, after I killed that deer, that I'd rushed the first shot, perhaps because I knew subconsciously that I had a quick second shot available. With a bolt gun I'd have taken more time and probably killed the buck with one bullet.

Pronghorn Rifles and Shooting

Pronghorn are taken at longer ranges than either of the two kinds of deer on the plains. From some of the stories about them you'd have to guess they're all taken at 400 yards in a 30-mile-an-hour wind. It is true, however, that most pronghorn are encountered at ranges of over 200 yards and that occasionally a skilled rifleman makes a shot at over 300. I have shot most of my pronghorn at between 250 and 300 yards.

Perhaps the best skill a prospective pronghorn hunter can develop is that of judging range. It's very helpful to know whether a pronghorn is 250 or 350 or 450 yards from the gun — a wrong guess will be a miss. Judging range, like making a million dollars, is a skill too few of us have, and I'd advise anyone going on his first pronghorn hunt either to hire a good guide who can judge range or to practice the skill. Perhaps the most-useful tool in that process is a rangefinder. There are some compact, practical models on the market, but they aren't always usable in every situation in the field; however, practice with one will enable a hunter to judge range more accurately.

There are two types of pronghorn hunters, and you should decide before your hunt which kind you'll be. One is the relative newcomer to the plains — he should perhaps restrict his shots to 250 yards, depending on his firearm. As I've said, probably 90% of all pronghorn are shot at under 300 yards (which many shooters will call anything from 400 yards to a mile). Anyone who's practiced from sitting and prone positions and shooting from a rest, and who has a scoped rifle using a load of at least 2700 fps muzzle velocity should be able to make shots up to that 250 yard range.

Shooting beyond that distance is sort of like finding a decent cheeseburger in Mexico — things get progressively more difficult

41

This pronghorn was taken at just under 300 yards with a .243 caliber Remington 700 rifle using a 6x scope – a flat-shooting, accurate combination, just what's needed for antelope.

42

the farther out you venture. Even the flattest-shooting rifles, when sighted-in correctly, will not keep their point of impact close to the point of aim much beyond 300 yards. The trajectory quickly becomes steep — past 400 yards the bullet starts downhill at such an angle that in some calibers a misjudgment of 50 yards can mean a complete miss. Ranges are harder to judge way out there, too, and wind becomes a factor — and more difficult to allow for than gravity's inevitable pull.

Wind always seems to blow in pronghorn country, as any resident of Casper, Wyoming will vehemently tell you, another reason to be up early, when the morning calm still has a slight hold on the air. At 400 yards an average prairie breeze of 10 mph will blow the bullet of an average rifle about a foot out of line — more than enough to miss or wound a pronghorn. A 20 mph wind (not at all unusual in such locales as Casper or Miles City, Montana) will blow the same bullet 24 inches off course.

To the uninitiated, it would seem relatively simple to carry a small wind gauge and, by virtue of a little practice shooting in windy weather, have a reliable guide to shooting the breezes (an image that has attacked me on the verge of sleep is that of a proper British pronghorn hunter, wearing a pith helmet and carrying a small anemometer, carefully stalking a distant buck). The problem is that wind, unlike gravity, is not always blowing at the same speed or even the same direction across that vast distance between you and your pronghorn. Experienced hunters try to observe wind signs downrange — how the grass is blowing, how the sage bends, even the tilt of the mirage in their scope — before making a shot. I use a handy little rule that I worked out with my own rifles, called the 3-6-12 rule, that's a rough gauge to shooting in the wind. With a 10 mph wind I allow 3 inches of windage at 200 yards, six at 300 and 12 at 400 (I just don't shoot past 400 yards if the wind is blowing). A five mph breeze will halve those figures; a 20 mph wind double them. Those estimates are just about exact for the rifles I use for pronghorn, which use bullets starting out at between 3000 and 3100 fps, which takes in 95% of all pronghorn calibers. But those figures are only a rough guide; shooting in the wind takes practice and sometimes a bit of intuition.

It is shooting past that 300-yard mark that separates the men-calibers from the boy-calibers. The best gun and load for pronghorn at long range is the one that drops least and blows around least. I've taken most of my pronghorn with the .243 and .270, and think that those are among the best. Other good pronghorn cartridges are the 6mm Remington, .25-06, .264 Winchester Magnum, .280 Remington (or its new loading, called the 7mm Express), 7mm Remington Magnum, and all the Weatherby Magnums from .240 through 7mm. All will give bullets of good ballistic coefficient (high efficiency in maintaining speed — usually streamlined bullets of at least moderate weight for their diameter) between 3000 and 3200 fps at the muzzle. Bullet drop and wind drift will be minimized.

The .243 and 6mm are just about identical in performance, and are perhaps better suited to hunting pronghorn than other big game. Both shoot bullets of 100 grains in factory loads (slightly heavier bullets are available for handloading) to just about 3000 fps, and are capable of cleanly killing any pronghorn in the West, even at 400 yards. Pronghorn are not large animals — a Primo Carnera of pronghorns might weigh 130-140 pounds on the hoof — and it doesn't take much penetration to go through a pronghorn's thin shoulder blade. The .243, frankly, is my favorite pronghorn cartridge, accurate, flat-shooting, mild-recoiling, and more than powerful enough for the job. Hunters who claim it isn't enough gun past 250 or 300 yards have usually never even used it at longer ranges — and often not at all. Every hunter I know who has really tried the .243 or the similar 6mm knows it is capable of any reasonable pronghorn shot.

The next rung up the ladder finds the .25-06, .257 Weatherby, .264 Winchester, .270 Winchester, and .280/7mm Express. All drive bullets of 120-150 grains at about 3000-3200 fps, and are also good pronghorn rifles. They kick slightly more than the .243 and 6mm, however, and are usually not so accurate. There are exceptions, however — most .25-06's are sharp and are available in heavy-barreled "varmint" versions that may just be the ultimate pronghorn guns. My own .270 will group with selected handloads into 2" or less at 300 yards. The .264 Magnum is the flattest-shooting of the group, actually just about the flattest-shooting factory big game cartridge there is, using an efficient bullet at high velocity. Its one problem is that it's often not as accurate as the other rounds listed.

The 7mm Magnums, of various shapes, represent to me the

upper limit of really good pronghorn cartridges. Their recoil is all most of us can really tolerate for the extended practice sessions necessary for the past-300 yard pronghorn hunter. They possess more power than is really necessary for pronghorn, but are flat-shooting and usually quite accurate.

Some hunters disagree with me (forgive them, for they know not what they do...), but I prefer the heaviest streamlined bullet I can find for my pronghorn rifles, in any caliber. Such bullets will start off slower than lighter bullets, but they shoot as flat or flatter past 300 yards and buck wind better than lighter weight bullets (though not by much). I use a 105-grain bullet, for instance, in the .243 and a 150-grain .270. The 150-grain .270 starts out at 2900 fps, and is only an inch or so lower at 300 yards than a 130 grain load starting out 235 fps faster. The only problem with some heavier bullets is that they don't expand well on pronghorn at extended ranges, being designed for slightly heavier game, but I haven't run into that problem. I must admit that they probably give me more of a psychological boost than anything.

More shooters use high-powered scopes for pronghorn than for any other big game. Some even use "varmint" scopes of 8x and up. I have a 6x scope on my .243, and it's excellent, but I doubt that it's really better than a 4x, or even a 3x. A reliable, optically-clear scope of 3x on up is probably adequate for any pronghorn situation. There isn't any harm in higher powers unless you happen to get a shorter-range running shot. Pronghorn are fast runners and require about twice as much lead as deer — the small field of view of a 10x scope may be too small to show both pronghorn and aiming point. I try to leave running pronghorn alone, however — they just move too fast to be sure of lead.

Big variable scopes the size of large salamis are popular these days, but they have some disadvantages. One is that they some-times don't shoot to exactly the same place if you turn the power ring. This isn't critical at short ranges, but for pronghorn hunting it's abominable. I wince every time I see some pronghorn hunter twisting the power ring on his new variable. If you use a variable, set it on one power and don't touch the damn thing.

Once you've put together your ideal pronghorn rifle, practice with it. If possible go out into some open country and take shots (using all due caution, of course) at rocks, patches of ground, or whatever. Shoot at long-range targets to truly find the trajectory of your gun and load — don't trust the trajectory tables from the factory; they, like television, are not real, no matter how close they come to convincing us they are. If you have a chronograph and can find out just how fast your loads travel in your gun, you can plot trajectory curve closely, but real range shooting should always be tried to make sure.

As long as you have an accurate scoped rifle that you know thoroughly and have sighted-in correctly, pronghorn aren't difficult to take out to 250 or 300 yards. Past that distance, however, they are all the challenge they are trumped up to be. Any hunter, whether new or experienced, should always consider carefully any shot past 300 yards — and if there's any doubt, pass it up.

Deer Rifles and Shooting

Deer in open country are not usually taken at as long range as pronghorn, though there are occasional instances of mule deer, especially, being sighted far across a coulee and their being no way to get closer. But deer (especially whitetails) are shot while moving more often than pronghorn, placing at least as much demand on hunter and rifle as long-range shooting.

A prairie whitetail bursting from the brush like a linebacker with antlers is a target that doesn't lend itself well to bullet placement. Like shooting in the wind, at long range, or when your lungs are heaving, shooting at moving game tends to increase possible error. Like shooting at flying birds, you have to lead the target, except at very short ranges; however, unlike shooting at birds, you have only one projectile instead of the several hundred of a shotgun. In spite of these difficulties, killing running deer cleanly is by no means impossible; at the shorter ranges at which running shots are usually taken (up to 150 yards) a practiced rifleman is almost as sure on moving deer as he is on stationary targets.

I have a couple of hunting partners in northeastern Montana, for instance, that are actually better shots on running than on standing deer. The reason is they've always hunted in that country and have taken most of their shots at running whitetail under 150 yards away. They've just never learned to shoot standing deer at longer ranges; they don't know how to assume a solid sitting position, and I don't think either of them knows anything

46

about shooting prone. A deer standing at 200 yards is a temptation to them to shoot quickly, offhand, as they do at running deer — and they miss. I, on the other hand, grew up shooting mule deer in semi-open canyon country in southwestern Montana and learned early how to cinch up a sling and to take advantage of any rest I could in order to cleanly chest-shoot a deer across a piney coulee. Perhaps I'd taken a couple of cracks at running deer before I moved to the prairie, but more in hope than with expertise.

Fortunately, northeastern Montana has plenty of jackrabbits, the big whitetailed variety. After my first few attempts at running deer produced nothing more than a few deer-snickers and some .270-cracked rocks, I decided I needed some practice. A sage flat a half-hour north of my home in Poplar provided a few afternoons of jackrabbit practice. After two or three sessions, I was able to hit or scare hell out of most running jacks out to about 200 yards — and a jackrabbit is about the size of a deer's chest cavity.

The lessons I learned were few, but important. First — it is usually faster and surer to adopt a quick sitting position on all but the closest shots at running deer (under 50 yards). A sitting position quickly steadies the rifle, while still allowing it to swing smoothly. Second — just as in shotgun shooting, follow-through with the firearm is of absolute importance. Any pause or stutter as the shot is released results in a miss behind the deer, or, even worse, a hit too far back in the guts or hams. My rule of thumb for leading deer is to hold on the shoulders of deer under 50 yards — the bullet will land anywhere from the shoulders back through the rear of the chest cavity — and then an additional foot of lead for each additional 50 yards of range. A deer at 100 yards requires about a foot of lead in front of his chest, at deer at 150 about two feet, a deer at 200 yards about three feet. I must emphasize that these are my estimates; as in shotgun shooting, lead looks different and is different for different shooters, because everyone swings and releases the shot at different rates. My two hunting partners insist they don't lead deer at all except at extra long ranges; I think this is because they have unusually quick swings, and shoot in what shotgunners call the "swing-through" method. Their guns are still moving rapidly as they swing through the deer, and the shot, though apparently released when the sights are "on" the deer, actually leaves the barrel when the rifle is pointing past the deer. When I shoot, I use the "sustained lead" method; I try to swing the rifle along steadily in front of the deer, keeping the apparent lead constant, until I squeeze the trigger. With either method, however, practice is paramount. Jackrabbits are ideal; otherwise a running deer setup at a target range or a tire rolled down a hill are the best substitutes. Whatever the method, you should practice as much as possible before trying to shoot running deer much past 50 yards.

The error inherent in pointing a rifle at a moving deer also means that accuracy is as important to open-country whitetail rifles as it is to pronghorn equipment. When you squeeze the trigger you want the bullet to strike as close as possible to where it's aimed. Many hunters believe that any old rifle able to hit a pie plate at 100 yards is adequate for shooting running deer — and it is, some of the time. A precision arm, however, helps compensate for shooter error, just as in long-range shooting.

Deer are bigger than pronghorn, too; a really large mule deer can dress out at 250 pounds, and whitetails can easily top 200. Either is two to three times as big as a buck pronghorn, and deer bones are proportionately larger. Add to this the possibility of having to drive your bullet through a shoulder blade or angle it through the chest of a slanting-away deer and you have the basic prescription for a larger rifle.

While the .243, 6mm and similar rifles are fine for pronghorn, they might be a bit light for shooting at really big or running deer. They don't always give the penetration needed, even with well-constructed bullets designed for deep penentration. I've taken about a dozen deer with the .243 and have never had any problems that weren't the result of my mistakes — but the field autopsies I've performed have convinced me that slightly larger cartridges are better for running deer. I've taken more big whitetail bucks with the .270 than with any other gun, but any rifle shooting a bullet of about 130-140 grains or more at 2700 fps or more is certainly adequate. I've also taken whitetail with the .308 using the 150-grain bullet and with the .30-06 with a 165-grain load; other good cartridges are the 7x57 and .280 Remington. The under-.30 caliber magnums work fine, too, but are handicapped because they hold one less round in the magazine than the "standard" rounds; sometimes that one cartridge is useful. The magnums also have more power and velocity than is really needed for whitetail, but they're fine long-range mule deer cartridges. If I were to pick one rifle for whitetails, it would be a .308 or 7x57; one for mule deer, a .270 or 7mm Magnum. Those are nit-picking choices, however, made only because when rifles are concerned, I like to pick nits. Any of the above rifles and others not mentioned will do for all deer hunting.

I've used scopes of 2½ through 6 power for open-country deer but have finally decided that those in the 3-4x class are ideal, having enough magnification for long shots and enough field of view for even the closest deer. Several whitetails and even one mule deer have fallen to my 4x-scoped .270 at 30-40 yards, and I've never had the slightest bit of problem picking them up in the scope.

Open-Country Archery Tackle

Open-country bowhunting is a relatively new sport, but the wide-open spaces limit the short-range bow. Most archers, therefore, confine their efforts to the denser stands of timber and brush along watercourses, more like "normal" bowhunting country than empty grama grass pastures and sage flats.

Though riverbottom hunting, with the bowman ensconced in a tree stand overlooking a deer trail, is the most successful and popular method of hunting big game with a bow on the plains, the hunter would be well advised to use a compound bow of at least 60 pounds draw weight for all-around plains hunting; unless he is willing to confine his hunting to deer. There are two primary reasons for this choice: pronghorn and elk. Pronghorn are hard-pursued by bowhunters across the plains (although the success rate is low), and compound bows will stretch the average archer's range just enough to make his hopes and real chances rise. In the hands of an expert archer, 60-70 pound compound bow shooting lightweight aluminum arrows can cleanly kill pronghorn out to 50 or 60 yards, and at shorter ranges provides a flatter trajectory than recurve bows and heavier fiberglass arrows, making a sure hit more sure for the average bowhunter.

Elk are also avidly pursued by open-country bowhunters, though in more restricted areas than pronghorn. In Montana, the plains elk areas are open to all archers merely through the purchase of an elk tag and bow permit — there are no lotteries such as the rifle hunters must face. As a result the bowhunting of elk has boomed since the early 1970's, roughly paralleling the nationwide bowhunting boom. Part of the reason for the popularity of these bow seasons, too, is that Montana's bow season is from mid-September through early October, coinciding with the elk bugling season. Somebody who can bugle a bit has a fair chance at calling a bull elk into bow range. A big animal like an elk needs all the bow you can bend.

Open-country mule deer also can present long shots, even though the deer are normally found in thicker cover during the warm bowhunting months. Juniper and berry thickets along steep hillsides hold most of the mulies at this time of year, and a hunter slowly still-hunting above the thickets can gain some medium range shots.

Whitetail hunters not only do well in the riverbottoms but occasionally can find deer by still-hunting the edges of riverbottom fields at dawn and dusk. Deer like to feed around the edges of fields because of the "edge" browse that the transition from forest to field provides. These shots, too, are likely to be on the long side. Some central Montana bowhunters I'm acquainted with hunt their whitetails from blinds constructed in the middle of stacks of hay bales. They sit and wait for deer to come out to feed on the edges of the fields.

I'd also advise a good bowsight for any bowhunter contemplating hunting the plains. Unsighted bows work well for shots up to 30 yards or so, but most hunters need a little guidance for the shots from 30 to 50. I prefer the simple pin-type sight, which is rugged and easily used, but several of my friends like the "rangefinder" type of sight, which supposedly encircles a deer's chest at various ranges. Since range estimation past 30 yards is as important to the bowhunter as past 300 is for the rifleman, they have a point.

Camouflage clothing and face makeup is even more important to the open-country hunter than the timber hunter, because he doesn't have the irregular shadows and outlines of branches and leaves to break up his outline. Duller shades of camouflage than many companies make are also useful to the plains hunter because of the predominant shade of autumn prairie grass or sagebrush. Old well-washed and faded camouflage clothing works well in these areas; or the camouflage designed for duck hunters in reeds is equally effective.

UPLAND GAME

Chapter Six: Sage Grouse

(Centrocercus urophasianus)

Two of my three companions were sure I was going mad. One
— my wife — had accepted the fact calmly and was attempting to
doze in the back seat of the Bronco. The other — her grandfather
— was becoming increasingly restless, as evidenced by the sput-
tering of his pipe. The believer was my Labrador, Gillis, who sat
quivering beside me in bird fever, as I gazed over the sage-lined
coulee below us.

The sun was almost down, and its colored light touched only
the tops of the eroded hills around us. I was beginning to doubt
myself — after all, we'd been sitting there for 15 minutes, hoping
(or, in the case of Linda and Ben, doubting) that the sage grouse
that had made the tracks around the little water hole below us
would show up for their evening drink. We were 300 yards away
from the water, parked on top of a hill; a couple of times each
minute I'd raise my binoculars to sweep the length of the sage
coulee above the water hole. Every time I did, Ben would sigh
loudly, evidencing his opinions of my hunting tactics. Why, he'd
hunted sage grouse for most of his 80 years and never heard of
anyone doing it with binoculars. Bird hunting to him was walking

The sage "hen" is the second-largest North American upland bird, smaller only than the wild turkey. These hunters have just taken a brace of typical five-to-six pound roosters from the shallow sage draw in the background.

the hills with dog and gun — none of this sitting and waiting.

The sun was almost gone; in another 15 minutes legal shooting would end. I raised the binoculars for a desperate look, knowing that if my plan failed, not only would we not dine on sage grouse in the near future, but Ben would let all the hunters he knew — and some he didn't — that his damn fool grandson-in-law had tried to hunt sage hens with field glasses.

For an instant, below me, I caught a flash of white in the dull sage. I wasn't sure, but adrenalin instantly made my breath come quicker. I didn't say anything, but kept the glasses on the coulee. Just as Ben stirred restlessly for the 20th time, and opened his mouth to say, "Well, we might as..."

"There they are!" Another flash of white along the sagebrush, and a dark, strutting, birdlike form was walking down the coulee toward the water.

"What?" Linda came out of her light nap. "Where?"

"You sure?" Ben asked, unable to see that far without binoculars.

For an answer I eased the door open and lifted my shotgun from the gun rack in the window. Gillis whined a little, then dropped to the ground beside me. Ben was out, too, already loading his 20-gauge pump.

"Heel up!" I hissed at Gillis, as he started to bound down the hill. He bowed his head and came to heel, prancing beside me, almost unable to control his enthusiasm.

I began to doubt myself again as we neared the dim coulee. What if I hadn't really seen anything? What if my desire to show my theory wasn't all that crazy had produced an imaginary shadow in the form of a sage grouse?

The coulee was about ten feet deep and twenty wide, bounded by big sagebrush. We walked along one edge, and I motioned Gillis into the brush. He jumped forward and pattered down into the tall sage. Perhaps two seconds later a giant bird flushed from the coulee below me and started to sail on four-foot wings out across the open grass. I raised the 20-gauge double, and when I shot, those incredibly long wings folded, collapsed upward as the bird fell. Gillis was there almost as it hit the ground; he mouthed it for a few moments, trying to find a good hold on the six-pound rooster, before carrying it across the coulee to me.

A sage grouse in a game vest makes you feel that you've

53

already hunted long enough. A couple of quail or even half-a-dozen doves are just a start, but a six-pound grouse is already quite a load. A three-bird limit (common in many sage grouse states) is enough to stagger a hunter on a warm day.

Sage grouse are the second-largest gallinaceous (chicken-like) game bird in North America; only the wild turkey is larger. A friend of mine once shot an old rooster that weighed an honest eight pounds before field dressing, and that bird fed seven people at dinner. An average mature rooster is slightly smaller than that — those I've weighed have usually been around 5½ pounds — but sage grouse also have longer wings for their size than any other grouse, and one in the air looks about as large as a young turkey. The hen sage grouse isn't nearly as big, but a mature female still outweighs a rooster pheasant. A sage grouse's heart alone is about the size of a plucked dove.

Paradoxically, good sage grouse country usually looks as though it wouldn't support any bird bigger than a sparrow. The big birds are able to attain their size in sere, semi-desert regions that are home only to coyotes, jackrabbits and pronghorn (not to mention occasional crazy hunters). And sometimes they are incredibly abundant in such apparently barren lands. Early settlers in the West told of flocks of hundreds of the big birds, and sage grouse — as well as other prairie grouse — were harvested and sold by the barrel to restaurants in the 19th century East. When the great populations of sage grouse declined in the early part of this century, it was easy to blame their disappearance on over-hunting, but game laws that prevented any kind of shooting still didn't bring the birds back. It wasn't until the 1930's, when drought and overgrazing gave new life to that perennial invader of the Western rangelands — sagebrush — that the sage grouse came back from the edge of extinction. Today the sage "hen" is in no danger, and hunting seasons are held over most of the West.

About three-quarters of the bird's diet is made up of sagebrush leaves. A sage grouse doesn't have a grinding gizzard like other grouse, and is only able to digest soft vegetation. Sagebrush is vital to its existence, and it just can't be any sagebrush. The severe winters of the northern plains will snow under the smaller varieties of sage, and only in regions where sagebrush is abundant and tall enough to grow above the winter snow cover are sage grouse common.

54

Those areas have shifted over the years. Sage grouse a hundred years ago roamed regions that had grown sagebrush for thousands of years, probably since the last ice age, about 12,000 years ago. Those vast areas of "worthless" sage were often eradicated by ranchers looking for more grazing land, and overgrazing by sheep and cattle in other areas that didn't have sagebrush allowed the opportunistic plant to move in. Today, better grazing practices and other factors have continued this sagebrush ebb and flow, and with it the ebb and flow of sage grouse.

Sagebrush regions are classified as northern desert, which means that water is scarce. Sage grouse will fly great distances (for grouse) to water, often up to several miles. They usually visit watering holes at least once a day, and often twice, in the morning and evening. It was this habit that I anticipated during that hunt with Linda and Ben. The waterholes most-frequented by the birds will have tracks — which you can't mistake for anything else — and droppings around the shore. In the vast sage plains of the West, you can walk for hours, hunting the way you would for pheasant or quail, and never run into a sage grouse. Often it's best to wait for them.

Early in the hunting season, which can start as early as late August, it's sometimes productive to follow sagey dry creeks. The birds will be under the sage during the day, out of the hot sun. If they haven't been hunted, they'll likely hold for a close shot, but they are also runners, like most open-country birds. A sage grouse can run fast for short distances, perhaps even rivaling the pheasant, but its standard foot-travel is a steady slower pace. A grouse will walk out ahead of you, perhaps at a rate just faster than yours, and keep it up for two or three miles. Chasing grouse loses excitement pretty quickly in the hot September sun.

Later in the season, the birds will start grouping. On one late-season hunt near Dillon, Montana, a cousin of mine and I must have run into four or five flocks of 30 to 50 birds each. The area was a flat, sagebrush-covered ranching valley, surrounded by high valleys leading to snowy mountains. The birds in this area spend the early part of fall scattered throughout the higher valleys, but as the snow line creeps down, they move into the valley bottom and are concentrated there. Earlier they are difficult to find; there's just too much country. In many areas they tend to concentrate as water sources dry up in the fall.

That same trip also offered a good demonstration of just how far those birds will fly. Each of the groups we flushed flew at least half a mile, farther than most upland birds will travel, and some we watched with binoculars until they disappeared. A few, I believe, are flying still.

When a sage grouse wants to move, it flies much higher off the ground than any other grouse. I've seen them at least 500 feet up. Once, while driving north of Billings, Montana, on a cold December day, I saw a flock of what appeared to be ducks flying over the prairie, perhaps a mile away. I was surprised, since by late December most of the waterfowl in eastern Montana are concentrated along the rivers, as all the open-country potholes are frozen. This flock of ducks was flying towards us, and as they flew closer, they looked less and less like ducks. They came over about 200 feet up, with a wind behind them, and kept going as far as I could track them — all sage grouse.

When you eat a sage grouse, you'll notice the large, dark-meated breast. Dark meat means many blood vessels supplying oxygen to working muscles, and sage grouse have the darkest, largest breast muscles of any upland bird.

They also, as I have mentioned earlier, have long wings. Most grouse have short stubby winds suited to rapid acceleration and short flights. The flush of a sage grouse compares to that of a quail the way the take-off of a cement truck contrasts with that of a Porsche. They just don't have the quick lift of smaller birds, though their top speed probably is equal to that of any other bird. Most of the challenge in sage grouse hunting lies in finding, not in shooting. The common shooting situation is flushing the big birds from sage clumps along dry washes. If they don't take off at a trot, you'll often see their heads through a screen of sage branches, peering like curious ostriches at the approaching hunter. They'll flush with a great flapping, skimmming the sage, often sitting down several yards farther on. The only way you can miss them is by thinking they're flying too slow. You have to lead them just like any other bird.

Immediately on shooting a sage grouse you should dress it, and if the intestinal tract has been punctured, rinse the body cavity thoroughly with fresh water. These birds are already sage-flavored because of their diet; a quick field-dressing will minimize the sagey flavor. Many native Westerners refuse to eat sage grouse at all, or will just eat the young, because of this flavor. An "old" grouse that has been properly dressed, however, retains just enough sage flavor for most palates. Just don't add any more sage! Some hunters also remove the sage-filled crop, but I haven't found that it makes much difference. What is important is to get the innards out.

Sage grouse, like the pronghorn, are among the last strictly plains game, and hunting them is a unique experience. In order to find them you have to come in close contact with the most-open of the wide-open spaces — and that's part of the reason people venture into the desert sage flats every fall.

Where to Go

Sage grouse, as their name suggests, like sagebrush, and wherever you find expanses of tall sagebrush you're likely to find expanses of tall sage birds. The heart of sage grouse country is Wyoming, as that state has more sagebrush than it probably desires, and sage grouse are especially prevalent in the south-central part of the state, from the Colorado border to the Rawlins area. Other good areas are the Bighorn Basin, between Cody and the Bighorn Mountains, and Fremont County, east of the Wind River Mountains.

Eastern Montana also has many good sage grouse areas, the best being south and east of Great Falls, south and east of Billings, and the area around Fort Peck Reservoir, especially south of the lake, between Winnett and Circle.

South Dakota has some sage grouse hunting in the northwest corner, and the southwest corner of adjacent North Dakota also offers grouse. Colorado's sage grouse hunting is primarily confined to the open country in the northern part of the state, especially the north-central portion. Alberta is about the northern limit of the birds, having a limited season in the extreme southeast, with a limit of two birds per season.

Across the Continental Divide, sage grouse are also found through southern Idaho, eastern Oregon, the northern two-thirds of flatter Utah, and even in a few spots in northeast California and eastern Washington. Oregon probably has the best sage grouse hunting west of the divide, just because it has the most sagebrush.

Chapter Seven:
Sharptailed Grouse

(Pediocetes phasianellus)

Greater & Lesser Prairie Chicken

(Tympanuchus cupido & T. paillidicinctus)

There were half-a-dozen of us, relaxing around the living room of a southeastern Montana ranch house, preparing for an early bedtime because opening day of the Montana upland game season was only eight hours away. We were discussing sharp-tailed grouse, the object of most eastern Montana hunters, and anyone listening would think we all had all the sharptails in Rosebud County rounded up in one of the corrals just outside the house, ready to brand. Everything pointed to a great opening day: high grouse populations, the first crisp weather of fall, several huge wheatfields all to ourselves, and some parts of the wheat stubble cut a little tall so the birds would feel secure and hold tightly. By the time we all went to bed, relaxed by a heavy steak dinner and post-meal bourbon, we knew morning would bring a great day.

We were up early, and the dogs — two black Labs and a young Viszla — pattered eagerly around the ranch yard in the half-light, knowing that something was up, since everyone in sight was carrying a shotgun. By the time the first pale-gold light touched the tips of the stubble, we were walking the fields in a long line, eyes aching for the first sight of those dark heads peering curiously above the yellow wheat.

Trouble was, we didn't get a bird. Somehow the sharptails didn't agree that perfect sharptail conditions prevailed over the stubble fields of the 66 Quarter Circle. Oh, we saw enough of them, mostly a quarter of a mile away and flying 100 feet high, heading for some far-away patch of brush. The closest we got all morning to a real live, honest-to-God sharptail was perhaps 75 yards. To top it off the Viszla, on his first Montana hunt, learned in the most difficult manner possible about porcupines and was rendered *hors de combat* for — the vet later said — about a week.

Considerably humbled, we headed back to the ranch in our two pickups, for a late breakfast. The conversation around the ham and eggs was full of moral outrage that mere sharptails would make such utter fools of the 100-plus years of grouse experience seated around that table.

"Them were the wildest goddamn birds I ever seen..."

"I don't think that one bunch set down until it reached Sarpy Crick..."

"Pass the ham..."

About noon we all headed out again, but in smaller, divergent groups. A friend and I spent three distinctly puzzling hours searching for birds. The temperature was in the 70's by the time we parked the pickup at the top of Camelback Ridge. The coulee below was colored by early fall, red and orange and yellow brush curving down toward Reservation Creek, two miles away. What the hell — it was a nice day, and we didn't have anythng else to do. Calling my Lab Gillis from the bed of the truck, we loaded our guns and started down.

Suddenly there were birds all around us, grabbing air with their wings, sounding the loud *clutlutlutl!* of sharptail alarm, skimming the top of the brush to land in thicker cover. I blew the first shot, unnerved by the explosion of unexpected sound, then caught a bird in the center of the second pattern, a trail of feathers following the falling grouse into a wild rose patch. My partner broke another bird's wing, and Gillis chased it down while I started for my bird.

59

We followed the coulee down toward the creek, putting up singles and doubles for half-a-mile. We each had a heavy five-bird limit in our game vests before we sweated back up to the truck.

That's the way it sometimes is with sharptail — you'll think you've got them all figured out, and they'll do something screwy. And once they've got you turned around, you end up expecting the unexpected. Why, any fool knows that the mid-day heat will usually find birds in the Camelback Coulee on opening day, but we were so confused by the wild birds of early morning we couldn't imagine the grouse would do anything the way they should.

Sharptailed grouse are the most common native gamebirds of the northern plains, though they also range up to Alaska and Hudson Bay. More adaptable than any other native bird, they can be found near wheatfields, in brushy draws, out in sagebrush, or along marshy riverbottoms.

Sharptail hunting seasons usually open in September across the northern plains. At that time of year the nights are chilly and daytime temperatures reach occasionally into the 80's; the birds are feeding primarily on grasshoppers and berries. They usually start September feeding predominantly on hoppers and begin October picking berries, as insect populations decline with cool weather. Food and cover are coincident at this time of year, grasshoppers in tall grass and berries in brushy coulees, and about the only time you'll catch sharptails in the open is during morning, when they might be found along a roadside picking up grit, or flying to water.

Favored berries are chokecherry, rosehip, wild currant and buffaloberry. It's easy to tell if birds are working a certain berry patch; the grass between the brush stems is beaten down by the passage of strutting birds into what the natives of the West quaintly call "chicken trails". (If you ask a Western rancher if he has any sharptails on his land and he says no, most of his cattle's tails are blunt, you might remember that most local people know sharptails as "chickens" or "prairie chickens.")

If you find "chicken trails," put your dog or yourself in the brush and walk out that patch. Brush shooting normally results in close flushes, but sometimes, especially in hot weather, it's hard to get the birds out. Most experienced sharptail hunters use flushing dogs of at least medium size; strong dogs are often needed to plow through cover to get the birds into the air.

Sharptails usually prefer a series of small berry patches strung along a coulee filled with shorter brush, within a half-mile or so of water. The most pleasant shooting occurs in the early season when a covey is flushed, scattering down along such a coulee. A nice half-hour can then be spent pushing up singles and doubles from each berry patch. The birds tend to hold tightly in warm weather after they've been flushed once, and are usually found right where they sit down.

As the season progresses and days become cooler, sharptails spend more time feeding on waste grain and weed seeds, though at mid-day they can still be found in berry patches, the gray-green buffaloberry thickets in particular, as buffaloberry sheds its leaves late. It's easier to see the birds out in the open, but harder to get a shot. It's at this time of year that you'll see pickup trucks cruising the wheatfields, one or two hunters standing in the bed, looking for those dark heads poking up over the stubble. It helps to know a rancher who's also a sharptail enthusiast, who'll cut parts of his grain a little higher from the ground. The taller the stubble, the better the chance the birds will hold for a shot; in tall wheat you'll often see them jerk their heads back down when they think they've been seen. Get over there quick or they'll run.

Fields with shallow dips that are the beginnings of coulees are also prime spots. It's harder to get a combine's sickle close to the ground when the field is curving this way and that, and the stubble will be several inches higher along the dips, leaving both cover and waste grain for the birds. At the edges of the fields, these dips also turn into deeper, brush-filled coulees, which are good spots for resting birds. If you don't find anything in the wheat, try the brush right next to it.

Often sharptails will flush wild in a field, but by following their flight (possible in open country) you can frequently spot where they put down, usually in slightly thicker cover such as knee-high "buckbrush" or wild rosebushes. Even then the follow-up can be frustrating, as the birds will often start trotting soon after they land. I've come over many a slight hill to have a sharptail flush a hundred yards before I expected to run into a bird, and then have the rest of the covey, clucking like scared setting hens, go over where I expected all of them to be.

61

I've stayed awake nights thinking of ways to get close to a wild November covey of sharptails. Too bad the birds ignore most of my ideas. I've tried everything — once I posted a couple of friends in a coulee that a certain covey of sharptails seemed to like to fly down once we'd jumped them from the field above. It worked, too, in a way; we all got shots, but the grouse had a 20-mile-an-hour tailwind and a good start. It was just like pass-shooting mallards with a good north wind pushing them south — except that none of us were used to leading sharptails 10 or 15 feet. I think we clipped one feather.

Late-season sharptails are most vulnerable in broken country, like hills cut by numerous deep coulees. On raw windy days they feed on grass and weed seeds just under the crests of sharp ridges, keeping out of the wind. They must be spotted first, either by jumping them and watching where they land or by carefully scanning the hills. The hunter then makes an into-the-wind sneak over the ridge, sometimes crouching over the last few yards, then standing and shooting. Normally one or two chances will be the most you'll get, and ranges will be long. One thing to remember is that the first bird aloft is often one of the farthest from the gun, as the nearer birds are frequently hidden under the ridge's crest. If the first bird up offers a chancy shot, it pays to wait for a possible closer flush.

The farther into the season you get (most states' run into November) the wilder the birds get, the farther they'll fly when flushed, and the bigger the coveys. Early season coveys run from two to 15 birds, but as the weather gets nastier, the small groups combine. Several years ago, on the last weekend of the season, a companion and I were ready to swear that all the sharptails had left the country. We'd driven over at least 50 square miles of prime territory in northeastern Montana near the Saskatchewan line and flushed exactly one jackrabbit. We were tired and ready to give up, when we drove over a ridge and I happened to see a sharptail's dim outline moving through some barren buckbrush. We stepped out of the pickup and called Gillis. The wind caught my door and slammed it shut; at the sound, 200 grouse arose *en masse*, the sound of their wings as loud as a low-flying airplane. We both shot wildly at a straggler and dropped it. I tried to keep track of the main covey as Gillis retrieved the dead grouse, but they were flying up in the jetstream somewhere, and I doubt if they stopped before they reached Canada. We both watched them with binoculars as they alternately flapped and set their wings, never slowing. In cases like that you just say bye-bye.

Prairie Chickens

The true prairie chickens — which are what many local hunters insist sharptails are — have not survived as well as the sharptail against the spread of agriculture. At one time they were found in enormous numbers across the flatlands, especially in the tall-grass prairie on the eastern edge of the grasslands. Ben Burshia says there were a few "striped chickens" in northeastern Montana when he was a young man, right after World War I, but that some "government men" — apparently Fish and Game people — trapped the last of them to transplant somewhere else. Most likely that transplant failed, because the prairie chickens disappeared in most localities not because of over-gunning (though that contributed to the decline) but because the grasslands had been plowed under. Most research has indicated that if more than half the grassland in a locale is converted to fields, the prairie chicken will have a hard time. Ben tells me that those "striped chickens" were always found in tall "sand" grass, a type of grass that is now rare in northeastern Montana.

Even though the greater and lesser prairie chickens are much less numerous than the sharptail, they are abundant enough in some areas for a hunting season. Many hunters have sentimental feelings about prairie chickens, as they do about sage grouse. They represent a vanished time, a different era, that we will never see again. The places they inhabit, like the great sage flats, are just tiny pockets of history scattered across the plains.

Aside from their dependence on grass, prairie chickens are much like sharptails — so much so, in fact, that they will interbreed. They're about the same size, slightly smaller than a hen pheasant, and they have similar feeding habits. They can be found in tall grass picking grasshoppers early in the fall, or feeding in the stubble of wheat and other small grains. They can normally be found in grassy draws, areas similar to the sharptail's cover except that the true chicken prefers grass to brush.

In some areas, hunters take morning and evening stands in grainfields and wait for prairie chickens to fly in to feed, an

Americanised version of pass shooting. It's possible that a spread of prairie chicken decoys might work wonders in such situations, though I don't known of anyone who's tried it.

I must confess that I haven't hunted the prairie chicken much, both because I'm one of those sentimentalists that see them as a trace of a vanished time, and because of a lack of opportunity. What little hunting I've done was in central "west river" South Dakota, just west of one of the great Missouri River reservoirs that split that state in half. The limit, as nearly as I can remember, was two birds. Directed by a local rancher to a grassy coulee just below a big pasture, I put up about half-a-dozen birds, taking my limit before the season was two hours old. From the top of that coulee, I could see perhaps 30 miles across the tan-green rolling hills, across the huge blue of the dammed-up Missouri to another stretch of hills on the other shore. Even after I had my limit, I kept walking the coulee and finally pushed out another pair of prairie chickens that flushed down toward the reservoir, sinking into the high grass a few hundred yards below me. I just watched them, wishing partially that there were no fences across those empty, grass-covered hills.

Where to Go

Sharptailed grouse are a northern bird, with five subspecies spread up from Nebraska to Canada and Alaska. The plains and prairie species are found mostly in the northern tier of states and the southern prairie provinces of Canada. They are general throughout eastern Montana, North Dakota, southeastern Alberta, southern Saskatchewan, and the southwestern corner of Manitoba, being most plentiful around grain-farming areas. The top hunting may be in Saskatchewan, but the hunting is excellent throughout the whole region.

Nebraska has good sharptail populations in the northwestern part of the state, as well as in the north-central Sand Hills region. The best South Dakota hunting is in the counties immediately west of the Missouri River, but grouse are found throughout the western part of the state, excluding the Black Hills. The best Wyoming hunting is in the northeastern part of the state, between the Bighorn Mountains and the Black Hills, though sharptail are also hunted in the Bighorn Basin and in the southeast.

There are also a few sharptail in the northwestern corner of Minnesota, though the hunting is poor. Minnesota and Manitoba are about the eastern edge of sharptail country.

Prairie chicken range is restricted. The best is in Nebraska, Kansas and Oklahoma, with South Dakota providing fair hunting. Nebraska's chickens are all the Greater subspecies, and the best hunting territory is in the Sand Hills; some hunting is also found in the southeastern and southwestern parts of the state. Kansas has both Greater and Lesser chickens, though the Lesser are confined to limited areas of southwest Kansas south of the Arkansas River and west of the Pratt and Barber county lines. The grasslands of the north-central part of the state provide good hunting for the Greater chicken. Oklahoma also has both varieties, with the Greater chickens being found throughout the northeast, and the Lesser in Roger Mills, Ellis, Woodward, and Beaver counties of the west.

New Mexico's best hunting is in the southeast for the Lesser chicken, while Texas has hunting in the Panhandle for both the Greater and Lesser.

There are also scattered pockets of remnant Greater prairie chicken populations in parts of Michigan, Wisconsin, Illinois, Indiana, Iowa, Missouri, Alberta, and Manitoba that are reminders of a time when the grass-chicken's range spread all the way east to Pennsylvania.

Chapter Eight:
Hungarian Partridge

(Perdix perdix)

The Hungarian, or gray, partridge is a civilized, egalitarian little game bird that believes that all — well, almost all — men should have a chance to hunt him. Probably this is the result of the Hun's long contact with humanity, having lived for thousands of years alongside various European versions of mankind. The Hun thrives best where we turn up the soil and plant our various domestic grasses, like wheat and barley, but he is also kind enough to venture into old farmyards, onto superhighway rights-of-way, or to live on the edge of town. I don't think there's anyone living on the northern plains that hasn't sometime, somewhere been startled by the flush of a dozen hand-sized rufous-tailed birds, whistling out of an unexpectedly small or civilized patch of brush.

Near my northeastern Montana home there are a couple of coveys that live close to town. One is known as the Dump Ground Covey and may be seen on late summer evenings parading through the roadside weeds along the quarter-mile dirt road leading to the town dump, just below the hill from the airport. In winter, this roadside cover drifts over in hard, wind-packed snow, and the same covey will sometimes be found on the highway shoulder on the edge of town, picking seeds and grit.

The other covey lives below the hill that my house stands on. Sometimes we find them a couple of hundred yards down the hill, and once or twice they've flown over the house to land in someone else's yard, only to leave again when they find out that this time they really are a little too close to man.

I've also been startled by Huns just below the treeline in central Montana, where altitude pushes the plains to the edge of the mountains. On one occasion I was just easing into the brush-limited frame of mind that is the ruffed grouse hunter's, walking up a two-rut road to a patch of aspens, when 15 Huns blew my mood all over the hillside with a noisy flush from some tall grass.

From the foregoing you might guess that the Hun can be found just about anywhere, anytime, and to a certain extent that's true, but he's also a homebody — or at least his descendants are — for the "same" covey of partridge can be found in essentially the same place year after year. On the plains this area may be as much as a mile long, but it's rarely anywhere near that wide. The prime place for a Hun covey, if you can be so specific about so widespread a bird, is a brushy dry creek or draw between grain-fields. Such a home gives the partridge everything they need: waste grain to supplement their diet through a cold winter, knee-high weeds or brush to nest in, and plenty of escape cover. Usually those little dry creeks contain some water in a few spots and also hold a berry patch or two to make the September days a little brighter.

Matching that description, there's a place I hunt every year. I usually drive by it several times before the season opens, from mid-summer on, out on various mushroom-hunting or berry-picking expeditions, and I can be sure that on one of those trips I'll see the covey, usually consisting at that time of year of a couple of parent birds and a passel of young ones. The little ones take off like feathered golf balls, each a tiny perfect imitation of the mother and father, right down to the miniature red tail, to sit down again within ten yards, unable to fly farther. Sometimes I'll venture after the covey on foot, just to watch the older birds go through their broken-wing act.

I've seen those little birds as late as September 1, and often when upland seasons open in the northern states, the size differential between old and young birds is strikingly obvious. Perhaps the season is too early in some areas, having long been set to match the yearly growth of other birds. Maybe we should wait and hunt Huns during pheasant time, in October — but this would only make a difference in the size of the birds we bag, not in populations.

I've heard many hunters talk of Huns being runners, and in some ways they are, but not like pheasants or even sage grouse. Perhaps, if hunted with a pointing dog, their tendencies become magnified. Huns early in the season will characteristically hold tight in cover, flushing over a hill in a burst of alarm and then running, after they sit down. They are also more willing to sit down in sparse grass than many other birds, and someone used to charging after a sharptail covey, assuming the birds have alighted in brush, will often find himself in the midst of a Hun covey going up from ankle-high grass, a hundred yards from any "real" cover. They'll eventually find their way into the edge of the brush, but on foot; they almost always sit down in the open and wend their way in pedestrian fashion toward taller vegetation.

I mention the adjustment of the sharptail hunter because often the two birds will be found together, especially in the early season, when heat and berry patches attract both birds to rose thickets and chokecherry patches. More than once I've put up both birds together and had a tough time trying to decide which to shoot first, a Hun or a grouse. Usually indecision ruins the chance, and I get neither.

Someone used to sharptails or pheasants will often find his shooting off when he happens on a covey of Huns. Many hunters talk about how fast "them Huns" are compared to the bigger birds, but for the most part that is an optical illusion; the birds only appear faster because they are smaller, though they do accelerate faster. Their top speed is little, if any, faster than a sharptail's; when the two are flushed from the same piece of brush, the sharptails will often come out first, being stronger and better able to beat their way through the branches, while the Huns come out slightly later, but catch the sharptails with a quick takeoff. Then they all fly off at about the same speed.

A hunter used to sharptails will also often think Huns are out of range when in fact they are well within 12-gauge power. Once you get used to them, they are not much harder to hit than sharptails or prairie chickens. You only think they are.

Once they've been shot at they become wild, but since they're much easier to follow than any other open-country bird, you can still take a few from a wild covey. Several years ago a writer friend named Norm Strung and I were hunting specifically for Huns north of Poplar. We'd found pheasants and sharptails, but it wasn't until mid-afternoon of that gray October day that we finally found some partridge. They flushed wild, before we even knew they were there, flying from a dry creek across a wide fallow field to a patch of low "buckbrush" on a hillside. We circled to the ridge above them and got within 75 yards before they flushed again and flew back down to the creek, to the original spot. By that time they were tired — like pheasants, they have relatively few blood vessels in their breast muscles, leaving them little endurance — and held tight for our two Labradors, who pushed the birds out right under Norm's gun. He shot two, his first double on Huns.

Norm told me once about an emigrant Hungarian count that lived near Norm's home in southwestern Montana. The count said that back in the "old country" they'd hunt partridge with horses, chasing after birds that had been flushed, which eventually would tire enough to be picked up by hand. Two or three fast flushes by foot hunters have the same effect, but not to the same extent!

Many northern plains birds can be found around abandoned farm buildings, especially early in the fall, right after grain harvests have been completed, but Huns are especially fond of old buildings. Most of those abandoned farms seen standing like gravestones on the plains are in use for grain storage, even if no one lives there. The windows of the houses and outbuildings are boarded up, and the old, empty shells are filled with wheat. There's normally a lot of spilled grain lying around the old farmyard, and Huns, in particular, are fond of living near the old buildings, probably because they've been picking over man's leavings for several thousand years, instead of for the mere century that most of our native western game has been forced to live with us.

When hunting a wheat farm, ask the farmer if it's OK if you hunt around his grain bins. Make sure you let him know you won't shoot a hole in one, and he'll likely let you know the location of every bin, which are usually scattered about the farm near various fields. The likely time for birds to be right out there pecking away is evening, but they'll be somewhere near, usually on the edge of a brush patch within a quarter of a mile of the bins, throughout the day.

Late in the season you're likely to see them out in the farmyard anytime, even during mid-day; they like to feed in the tall weeds on the lee sides of buildings once the weather gets really cold. Even on the prairies of Canada this doesn't usually happen until December, but in some areas the hunting season lasts until then.

As I noted before, however, Huns can be found anywhere, anytime. I almost ran over a covey once on an exit ramp of Interstate 90 on the edge of Butte, Montana, and have had them flurry out of thick rosebushes when I was hunting riverbottom pheasants in North Dakota.

Probably the best way — but in some ways the hardest — of finding Huns is by asking locals if there are any around. This can get to be a game of 20 Questions, however. In my area of Montana many of the locals call sharptailed grouse "chickens" and Huns "quail". They've heard that quail are small birds so anything smaller than a sharptail is a quail. (I don't know what they'd call the birds in western Oklahoma — maybe "partridge" and "grouse".) It is sometimes hard to sift through colloquial misnomers; an outdoor writer named Ron Rau found Huns in northern Alberta masquerading under the alias of "blue ruffled grouse." Most of the time it's easiest to describe the birds you're looking for, which usually are grayish with brick-red tails, or the smallest bird in the country, though occasionally, after a series of mild winters, the northern range of the bobwhite will overlap the southern range of the Hun. There's usually someone around, though, who remembers when cousin Bill ground-sluiced a bunch of "quail" or even a sporting-goods salesman who knows them by their right name. If you look hard enough you'll find them.

Where to Go

Since the first plains Hungarian partridge releases were made in eastern Montana, southern Alberta and the Dakotas in the early part of this century, the little bird has spread himself well across the northern grain belt. His main range is from the Montana, Alberta, and Wyoming Rockies east to western Minnesota, south to the southern border of South Dakota, and north through the grain-growing portions of the prairie provinces. There are also

70

healthy populations on the plains of Washington, Oregon, southern Idaho, and northern Nevada.

The Hun is a grain bird, plain and simple, and the greatest populations will be found in the grain-growing parts of those states, though the Hun is also an adaptable bird that can crop up almost anywhere. Northern Montana is wheat country and has more birds than the southern, grazing part of the state, where Huns hang around the creekbottoms for the most part. Northern and western North Dakota are better than the southeastern portion, but hunting is generally good throughout the state. The farm areas of eastern South Dakota are best, the west mainly being grazing land, though there are areas that are wheat centers, and these have Huns. Wyoming's best hunting is in the northeast and north-central valleys.

Iowa's Huns are restricted to the northwestern corner of the state, and Minnesota's to the west and south. Hunting is generally good throughout the plains portions of Alberta and Saskatchewan, but the birds are limited mostly to the southwestern corner of Manitoba.

JOHN BARSNESS

The Hun is the northern plains version of the bobwhite, being home-loving, gregarious and capable of quick acceleration.

Typical plains pheasant habitat in grazing country is thick brush along watercourses. Pheasants require thicker cover than most other open-country birds.

Chapter Nine:
Ringnecked Pheasant
(Phasianus colchicus)

I grew up in western Montana's Gallatin Valley, where there aren't many pheasants, and so came late to hunting the big ringnecked birds. I killed my first when I was 16, and even then it wasn't exactly the kind of experience you'd find in the monthly outdoor magazines. It was a hen, and I killed it with a pickup truck in the middle of January. The damn thing flew into my left headlight. I ate it — and couldn't see why people raved over pheasant meat. It was tougher than the round steaks off an old mule, and besides, it was full of broken bones. Not your *corpus delectable..*

With that background information, you won't be surprised that I didn't kill another pheasant until four years later. I was living in South Dakota, the legendary pheasant state (though this was well after the big pheasant years in the '50's and '60's) and felt some obligation to try to find a rooster or two, partly because I kept hearing voices. "What? You lived in South Dakota and never hunted pheasants? Are you crazy?" Well, the truth is I just about was crazy. I was working in the state psychiatric hospital in Yankton, in the southeastern part of the state, when one of my co-workers asked me if I'd help him "guide" some brain surgeons — friends of his father, a local doctor — who were flying in from Kentucky for opening day. I think my friend really needed the use of my pickup truck, but anyway I said OK, and at 10 o'clock of opening day morning we were in the motel, trying to roust the brain surgeons from their hangovers. They'd spent the night playing cards and drinking beer, like caricatures of visiting hunters everywhere. The season didn't open until noon, a curious custom often common in pheasant states; perhaps some early fish and game legislator in one of the corn states decided he didn't want to get up early on opening morning to beat the rest of the crowd and hence decreed high noon as blast-off time. At any rate, the late starting time allowed our collection of brain surgeons to gulp some hangover remedies and un-blear their eyes for the test against the mighty ringneck.

We tromped the fields for most of that wet-gray day. By mid-afternoon we had a few birds and the brain surgeons were well on their way to another hangover, having engaged in the unique custom of tromping back to my pickup after every successful corn-field drive to have one of the beers they'd stashed in the cooler. As sunset drew near, I was becoming decidedly nervous, having neither a pheasant nor any idea when one of the surgeons might wave a shotgun past my head. The next bird that got up I killed very dead, then suggesting that, since every one of us had a bird, we go celebrate in a local bar — there the surgeons would have to leave their guns at the door.

That second pheasant experience might well have cured me of cornfield madness forever, but somehow I pulled through. Partly because my wife and that pheasant combined to make a wonderful meal, I have since become an addicted follower of the long-tailed bird.

The pheasant can be found anywhere in the northern United States and southern Canada where there's some cover, but the northern plains and prairie states are the heart of his stamping grounds. South Dakota was indeed the "Pheasant Capital of the World," as it proclaimed itself in the '50's and '60's. The Soil Bank Program, which endeavored to keep the prairies from blowing away and covering Toledo as they had during The Great Depression, provided lots of cover for the birds, and they multiplied and replenished the earth, or at least that portion of the earth within a two-day drive of Mitchell, South Dakota. North Dakota, Nebraska, and Iowa also had millions of pheasants, and the surrounding states a larger-than-normal allotment. When I lived in South Dakota, I talked to many hunters who'd been around during that era , and they told of getting a six- or eight-bird limit within an hour of "opening noon," taking them back to town, and then going out to get another limit before sunset. In some years, as many as 20 million pheasants were harvested in South Dakota alone.

Occasionally you'll still find some dinosaur around who'll tell you viciously that such shooting killed off the Dakota pheasants (or maybe it was the damn foxes), but we modern, sophisticated hunters all know that the pheasant population died because the Soil Bank Program died. Farmers started plowing their land to the edges of the fields, taking away weedy nesting cover. Some states even began to mow, burn, or spray their roadside ditches, which provide nesting cover for 20 to 30% of the pheasants in some areas. The "Pheasant Capital of the World" became more like the "Pheasant County Seat." Instead of 20 million pheasants being harvested every year, perhaps a million or fewer were bagged. Some biologists guessed that there were only 20 million birds come fall in the whole state. Neighboring states had similar declines.

Since then, various techniques have been tried to increase the numbers of pheasants, as they provided not only a lot of hunting and good meals during their heyday but millions of bucks in income from visiting hunters. South Dakota in 1976 approved a Pheasant Restoration Act, which allocates money to be spent on "cropland retirement" to create pheasant cover, along with re-stocking and predator control. The initial plan is for 6500 acres of additional pheasant cover a year. The results so far have been encouraging, but it's likely we'll never again see a pheasant population like that of the golden age.

Pheasant hunting is still remarkably good from Iowa through eastern Montana, and from Kansas up through the southern prairie provinces, though limits have been cut from the six- or eight-bird bags of the boom years to around three birds. Pheasant habitat in this region ranges from the cornfields of Iowa, south-eastern South Dakota, eastern Nebraska and Kansas to the wheat country farther west and finally to the cover along the small creeks and rivers of grazing land. Pheasant hunting tactics vary from place to place, none being entirely successful with this running, wary bird.

Pheasant come closer than any other gamebird to matching the whitetailed deer in sheer survival abilitty. They live closer to man than any other wild gamebird, even the Hungarian partridge. I once worked for a rancher in eastern Montana; the first day out on the job, doing some general work around the ranch yard, I frantically pointed to three or four rooster pheasants strutting around the fuel tanks. The rancher gave me a bored look and said those were the "tame" pheasants. I found he didn't mean they'd been raised in the chicken coop but that they were just the pheasants hanging around the yard. He didn't allow anyone to hunt them; pheasant shooting wasn't allowed within a hundred yards or so of the ranch yard fence. Often it was most successful a hundred yards from that fence.

I knew several corn farmers in South Dakota that "baited" birds with a leftover stand of corn near the house, and on opening day they'd harvest a limit of corn-fattened pheasants. Most of us, however, don't have either a ranch yard or a corn patch, so we have to resort to less practical tactics to get a pheasant dinner.

In corn country, especially during the big years, it was common to drive a field with several hunters. Three or four men would stand at the end of a field to block the birds that tried to run out. The drivers would walk down the rows of corn, whether standing or stubble, and the birds, finding themselves hemmed in by standers and drivers, would fly in a raucous explosion of psychedelic color as the drivers neared the end of the field. Stories of the "old days" tell of a hundred roosters in the air; nowadays three or four is a good flush. Anyway, driving is a good method if there are more than a few birds around, though you have to be sure of your shooting partners. I had become tenterhook-nervous at the ends of the brain surgeon drives. I was younger then and more easily led astray; today I wouldn't hunt with the SOB's.

Driving is also a good method, along a fence row or hedge, and especially productive when only two or three hunters are together. Ideally, two of the hunters should walk each side of the row, trying to drive the birds toward the end, where a stander is waiting. With only two hunters, there can be only one driver, and sometimes his best bird-dog efforts will reward him with the sight of a long-tailed rooster taking off across country on the other side of the row.

76

The drive is a good method for dogless hunters, and can even work in stubble fields. It is amazing how a bigger-than-a-breadbox bird like a rooster pheasant, colored like a pack of Crayolas, can hide in corn stubble only six inches high, but they can. I actually watched one of those brain surgeons step over a rooster in a stubble-field drive. The bird flushed after the "hunter" had taken a few more steps, and everyone whirled like a high school band to take a shot. The bird escaped unscathed.

Unless you can get a few hunters together or the pheasants are really abundant, a dog is a tremendous help. (Or you can use a method commonly employed by "locals" in pheasant states, called road hunting: you drive the back roads, looking for pheasants in ditches, and then blast them from the car window. Not exactly sporting or even legal, but effective if you somehow can't force yourself to walk 20 feet.) At the approach of any predator, including man, a pheasant's immediate reaction is to imitate a jogger, taking off through the brush and crashing through rosebushes, leaves, and weeds like a miniature feathered tank. The best pheasant dogs can pursue in such cover, getting close enough to a running bird to make it fly.

A good retriever is also helpful in rounding up the casualties. Pheasant are as tough as elk and sometimes seem twice as fast, and a rooster only wing-shot will hit the ground and accelerate. Unless there's a good dog near who can run like Secretariat, you're not likely to collect that bird. There are some hunters that can run down wounded roosters on open ground — I watched a brother-in-law of mine do it once — but unless the path is clear and you're close, you don't have a chance. And I've never met a human hunter with a decent nose, either.

In heavy cover, even dogs will just make pheasants run faster. If the bird can't be reached, he just won't fly. In thick cover, the birds will wait you out, but their stalling can be used against them. There's a stretch of alder, rose bushes, and willow that borders on a couple of wheatfields along the Poplar River, in Montana. A big patch of buffaloberry stands at one end of this quarter-mile-long brushy stretch. Late afternoon will often find the birds in the buffaloberry. The last time I hunted it they were there, and Gillis rousted out half-a-dozen hens and some roosters. I didn't get a clear shot as the birds scattered through the alder and chest-high roses, and even though I saw the birds flushing and running in the cover as we worked along the river, I didn't get another shot. Finally, scratched and weary, Gillis and I worked our way to the end of the brush, along a six-foot-high bank above the river. The cover thins there, to shin-high roses, and the birds either have to fly across the river or run across a wheatfield. They don't like to do either. We stood there for perhaps two minutes, listening to doves flutter nervously in the thickets and ourselves panting furiously, before a rooster lost his nerve and came squawking out of the low roses 30 yards away. For once I shot well and killed him so cleanly that his tail stuck straight up in the air out of the roses, giving Gillis a handy marker for the retrieving job. At the shot, a couple of hens flushed across the river, into some brush on the other side.

Pheasants have some definite daily rhythms that are just certain enough to make you think you can take advantage of them. One is that they'll usually feed around mid-morning and again in mid-afternoon. Those are the best times to find birds in stubble or berry thickets. Wheat country pheasants are fond of waste wheat, but are damnably hard to catch in the stubble, unlike the corn country birds. Late December usually finds a skiff of hard snow over the wheat stubble in southern Canada, Montana, and North Dakota, and on sunny days there'll often be more than one pheasant far out in the middle of a field, pecking away at wheat kernels where the snow has been blown away. Montana's pheasant season sometimes stays open until December, and more than once I've wished the law allowed the use of a .22 for those birds, as it does for mountain grouse. There's just no way to get close to them. Occasionally you can chase them into a coulee and flush them there, but usually once you get their legs warmed up they just keep going in the direction they started in.

One of the most dependable pheasant habits in dry wheat country is their noon watering routine. Sometime between 11 and one o'clock they'll want a drink during the warm days of the early season, and I never pass a brush-rimmed waterhole in dry country without letting Gillis make a reconnaissance tour. Ben Burshia always told me that pheasants are "around water at noon," but I never was convinced of it until one day when we were out after whitetailed deer and any birds we could find, near Medicine Lake, Montana. It was a warm day in late October, and the dogs were hot in the windowed camper shell of the pickup.

We stopped at a little water hole to let them drink. I opened the door of the camper, and the dogs eagerly rushed toward the water while I proceeded to heed nature's call. Both the dogs and I were startled when half-a-dozen pheasants blasted out of the brush on the water's edge. Since then I've never let the dogs out for a noontime drink without having a shotgun ready.

When wheat country pheasants aren't feeding or drinking, they'll usually be in thick cover close to the stubble fields. It has to be thick, too; sharptailed grouse and Hungarian partridge can be found in knee-high buckbrush on the edges of wheatfields, but pheasants need more protection. Most will be found along the little watercourses, but scattered populations are found wherever there's wheat and tall cover. The best time to try such spots is later afternoon, just as they're about to roost.

Pheasants are also fond of the edges of marshes. The backwaters and sloughs of the larger prairie rivers are often edged with pheasants. There's one long slough of the Montana Missouri that I've hunted off and on for several years. It's an old cutoff channel of the river, perhaps two miles long, that has created a "peninsula", covered with tules, cattails, and some cottonwood timber. The inland shore of the slough is also covered with reeds and bordered by wheat and barley fields. Pheasants roost in the tall reeds, which in most places on the peninsula are seven or eight feet high, and fly across the slough to feed in the fields. On a typical autumn afternoon they'll feed until about three o'clock, then walk into the reeds along the shore to dust and digest for a while before flying across the slough to the reeds on the peninsula. There's a period of about an hour where a hunter with a dog can walk along that strip of field-bordered reeds and be pretty sure of putting up at least a couple of roosters. Because the reeds are so thick, the birds tend to fly instead of run, flushing out over the water. A successful shot implies a retrieving dog.

I've hunted that strip a lot, and if I get there too early or too late, I have trouble. Too early means that the birds are still feeding in the stubble, and they'll flush well out of range and fly directly across to the tall reeds on the peninsula. Too late and they'll have already rested and will have flown to the peninsula. It is possible to hunt the birds in the 20-acre patch of reeds in the peninsula, because deer keep paths open through the six- to eight-foot vegetation, but it's difficult. The birds will flush for just a moment above the tall reeds, then dive back into them, offering just a quick shot. And without a dog it's impossible to retrieve a wounded bird.

In many states pheasant hunting lasts well into fall, and an early snow can either help or hinder matters. If the snow is light, it is usually an advantage for the hunter, offering quieter footing, and sure knowledge, through tracks, of where birds are. Both hunter and dog can get closer to the birds before alarming them. The louder you are, the more apt the birds are to run. Startled at close range, they're likely to flush.

Pheasants are also more likely to hold on bitterly cold days. I was hunting with a couple friends once in early December, on a ranch in the grazing country of southwestern Montana. We were working a little creek, two of us on one side and one on the other, with two Labradors working the brush in between. There were about six or eight inches of fresh soft snow on the gound, and we were picking up a few fresh tracks. Gillis followed one track into thick brush and put a rooster out, which flew away from us. We heard our companion shooting on the other side of the brush, and then a shout of success. Gillis came out of the brush, trying to find the bird, and trotted up to the edge of the creek's bank to me. Suddenly he dropped his head and started sniffing the empty snow about five feet from me and my companion. For a moment I thought he was crazy — there weren't any tracks — but a moment later I was sprayed with snow and so startled that I almost shot the hen pheasant that burst out of the snow, having dug itself under for insulation against the sub-zero night.

More than any other prairie or plains gamebird the pheasant's habits vary with the terrain. If you put an experienced sharptail or sage grouse hunter in new country, he'll probably be able to find some birds, but knowledge of local conditions and the best times and ways to hunt are invaluable to the pheasant hunter. It took me two or three years of working that slough and peninsula along the Missouri before I'd worked it out that the birds could be most effectively hunted during that one afternoon hour. And that strip of brush along the Poplar River where I drive the birds to one end and wait can only be effectively worked in that direction; if the birds are chased the other way, they'll run across an opening to the next patch of cover and keep on going. And though there are certain general rules about pheasant daily routines and the places

80

they like to hide, they can be quick to change their habits. Again, like whitetailed deer in hard-hunted country, they'll be somewhere around, and often closer than you think, but they'll pick places that are harder and harder to hunt. There's a patch of "badlands" above the Missouri near my home in Poplar that rises for three or four miles from the river before leveling off into a plateau. The plateau is topped with grainfields, and the brush patches below the fields are prime spots for pheasants. For a long time anybody in the area hunted there when he felt a roaring need for a pheasant dinner. Quickly the hunting got tougher and then almost ceased. Patches of thick buffaloberry that had always been prime pheasant spots came up barren. Most of the hunters just wrote the area off as "shot out," but I couldn't believe that — it's just about impossible to completely clear an area of pheasants by hunting pressure alone. Since the past few winters had been unusually mild, preventing any severe winter-kill, I decided to explore these badlands. I worked places that looked like good bighorn country, sometimes barely able to stay upright on the gumbo knobs. Finally, late in the afternoon, I flushed a dozen roosters from a juniper patch. They were all well out of range, flying raucously downhill toward the Missouri, three miles away and 600 feet below me. Since it was all downhill, they just glided, going further than I'd ever seen pheasants fly before. After I finally lost sight of the last one, I made the scrambling climb back up the face of the badlands, reassured that the average pheasant is entirely able to outsmart the average hunter.

Where to Go

Pheasants, like Hungarian partridge, are grain-country birds, though they can also be found far out in the badlands, miles from the nearest wheatfield. Their main range goes farther south than that of the Hun, down into Nebraska, Kansas, Utah, and even parts of New Mexico, but runs north about the same distance, across the southern halves of Alberta and Saskatchewan. They're also found, like the Hun, in the valleys of Oregon (where they were first successfully introduced from Asia in 1881), Washington, Idaho, and extreme northern California.

The very northern tip of the Texas Panhandle, the Oklahoma Panhandle, and parts of eastern New Mexico offer limited pheas-

81

ant hunting, that country being a bit south of really good pheasant habitat. Hunting perks up as you head north to Kansas, Nebraska, and eastern Colorado. All of Kansas except the extreme southeast offers good pheasant hunting. Nebraska's shooting is best in the south and east, with one high concentration of birds around Alliance, in the northwest. Colorado's pheasants are found all through the eastern third of the state, but are most common in the southeast and northeast.

Both North and South Dakota's hunting is best in the eastern parts of each state, though birds are found throughout both Dakotas. Wyoming's best pheasant areas are around Torrington, in the southeast; in the Bighorn Basin, in the north-central, and in Sheridan County, on the eastern edge of the Bighorn Mountains. Montana's hunting is best in the northeast, but birds are found in almost all the eastern two-thirds of the state, being most scarce in the central area.

The southern third of Saskatchewan is good pheasant country, while Alberta holds a one-week season for residents only.

NORM STRUNG

An Oklahoma bobwhite takes off in typical plains bobwhite country. Western quail country is not as intensively agricultural as eastern quail habitat, and the birds are often found in wide-open grazing land.

82

Chapter Ten:
Bobwhite Quail & Scaled Quail
(Colinus virginianus & Callipepla squamata)

It does seem like a long time ago when I lived in South Dakota, but it has been only six years. Perhaps it feels so long ago because the part of the state I lived in seems so far away. It wasn't the South Dakota I, growing up in Montana, was acquainted with, not the Black Hills and the high plains of the western part of the state. The part of the state I lived in was one of cornfields, where a big "hill" took two or even three minutes to climb and where a hunter was rarely out of sight of a farmhouse; where solid citizens venture to nearby Sioux City, Iowa, for a big night on the town; where they can go out to mow the lawn and see Nebraska (more cornfields), if they live down on the Missouri, as I did; where South Dakota is catfish and cricket country.

It shouldn't have surprised me, then, walking one morning in October casually along a farm road that ran between a Missouri bottomland field and the thick brush and timber beside the field, when a flock of little birds that seemed no bigger than western meadowlarks buzzed like deerflies out of the stubble and into the brush. It shouldn't have surprised me, but it did. What's more, I had in my hands a 20 gauge shotgun (about to be used on a duck slough a half-mile ahead) and a valid South Dakota bird license in my pocket. I just stared at the vanished-bird space in the cool air. I'd been introduced, albeit informally, to the bobwhite quail.

The Oklahoma-Kansas region may just be the best bobwhite area in North America.

There are about four or five counties in that humid, extreme middle-western section of South Dakota that occasionally harbor huntable populations of bobwhites. Several mild winters in a row will boost their numbers enough so that hunting — if not outstanding to a Kansas or Oklahoma quail man — is at least respectable. A couple of harsh winters, on the other hand, will turn all the upland hunters down there in Corn Country away from quail and into the South Dakota National Bird, the pheasant.

Most of all, I guess, it was the size and speed of the quail that amazed me. After all, I'd just moved from Montana, where grouse sometimes weigh seven or eight pounds, where Hungarian partridge are often disdained by local hunters out after a "decent meal," and where nobody shoots those "cute little doves." In my perception, those quail were a hell of a lot smaller than any Hun I'd ever seen and not much bigger than a dove. But I'd heard strange rumors that people actually did hunt quail and that some people (especially those Southerners) really like to.

If I recall correctly, I actually did shoot one bird out of that covey that fall, but for some reason can't remember eating it, something that is surprising because I was poor at the time and because quail rank right up there with pheasant and ruffed grouse as a gustatory idyll. I think it was mostly luck that allowed me to point a shotgun in the right direction for a clean kill, because back then I had a hard time hitting sharptailed grouse on the ground. Since then, however, I've hunted the bobwhite a few more times, and in areas more amenable to quail. I'm not going to set myself up as a quail expert, because I haven't hunted them enough, but when I have hunted them, I've gone along with real quail hunters and listened closely to what they said.

It's surprising, especially to people from the South, that there are so many damn quail across the midlands of our country. Some even say that Kansas and Oklahoma are quail heaven, and certainly the recent harvest figures show that Kansas is right up there among quail states. The reasons are primarily tied to the changes in agriculture over the past several decades. Quail are denizens of grasslands, and also need cover. They thrive best where there is plenty of food (seeds) and enough cover for nesting and resting. Man's grasses — grains — provide much more nutritious and abundant food for quail than any natural grass, and when both grain and nearby cover are abundant, in the right

85

climate (not too much snow so the grass doesn't get covered up in winter), quail thrive. Prior to the last World War, there were many more small farms farther east and south, in traditional quail country, which provided small fields between areas of cover, and quail hunting was excellent. As "efficient" modern agriculture took over, however, the hedgerows, small stands of brush and timber, and weedy edges of fields were eliminated, and so was quail cover. The plains of Kansas, Oklahoma, and other states on the western edges of the plains aren't so flat as the prairies further east, and so our modern "clean" farming practices haven't been able to gobble up the last bit of cover. And modern farm practices also haven't been able to eliminate the signs of our old farming — the great gullies and washouts created across the Dust Bowl region during the '30's. In many parts of Oklahoma and Texas, those deep, jagged gashes in the earth provide edge cover for quail.

At any rate, there are lots of quail on the southern plains and prairies. An Oklahoma quail hunt may lack the tradition of a mule-drawn wagon hunt in Georgia, but many quail enthusiasts down there like their "pointin' dawgs," and the limits are usually liberal. You may have to walk farther than you would on a southeastern quail plantation, but you're likely to find as many or more birds.

Quail are the dog man's delight, and many quail hunters are really after an afternoon of dog admiration rather than any actual hunting. The only other kind of hunting that I've found to match the last few seconds of walking up behind a good pointing dog who's locked onto a little piece of quail cover is working a coulee that has a good chance of holding half-a-dozen whitetailed deer. In both cases, the valves in your heart are doing something you wish they wouldn't, your hands are beginning to hurt from grasping the gun so hard, and when there is action, you often react too quickly.

Quail hunting is usually a simple process, the real challenges and enjoyments being in dog work and shooting. Quail (like almost every other organism higher than an amoeba on the evolutionary scale) feed in the morning and evening. In agricultural country, this means hunting the edges of fields close to cover during those times, letting the dog(s) work ahead, and then slipping up behind the point for the flush. In some of the western

Kansas and Oklahoma country, it means working the edges of the huge washouts, or perhaps of brush, in grazing country. During mid-day, most traditional hunters lounge around for a good long lunch, lie, remember other hunts, and just wait for afternoon. (In Oklahoma they drink a lot of Pepsi-Cola.) Some other hunters, however, also hunt the brush patches during the middle of the day and usually do well. This is more akin to hunting ruffed grouse, with the hunter following the dog through nasty stuff and shooting lightning quick at disappearing forms, but in many hard-hunted areas, brush-hunting can provide as much hunting as the traditional methods.

Quail, like Hungarian partridge, are home-loving birds; and a covey that's found in a certain area will be there again, even more so than Hun coveys. That first covey I ever found in South Dakota was always right there along that field road, within 100 yards or so of the place I originally flushed them, and quail hunters everywhere speak of the "corner covey" or the "Old House covey." Most quail hunters know their favorite places and coveys well, and for those of us who don't live in bobwhite country our best bet when we want to hunt quail is to become friends with someone who does know the area, and then follow him around — especially if he owns one or two good pointing dogs.

That's my general practice when I hunt quail, but the biggest problem I have is in shooting. I'm worst on the first two or three coveys. The main problem is the optical illusion — someone used to targets the size of basketballs (sage grouse) or even ripe canteloupes (sharptailed grouse) will always think quail are moving faster and are farther away than they really are, especially in the excitement and adrenalin of the flush. I usually carry a light 20 gauge side-by-side, and when I've used up both barrels on the first covey and the birds are still less than 20 yards out, I know I've screwed up. The next time I'll be better, and after a while I've adjusted, though no one's ever said shooting quail is easy. I don't think they fly any faster than any other bird, but they accelerate fast. Also, they usually offer straight going-away or slightly angling shots, so when I coldly analyze the last covey, I can never figure out why I have empty shells in my pocket and no quail.

Scaled Quail

Scaled quail, or "blue" quail, are another story entirely, if I can believe my friends. They are the only kind of plains game in this book that I've never hunted, and I have no desire to do so, from what I've gleaned from some New Mexico and Texas friends.

Scaled quail live in much more arid regions than the bobwhite, though they overlap in some areas. They are primarily a bird of the Southwest, but they range up across the grasslands of Colorado and Kansas, and are partially, at least, a plains bird. A cousin-in-law who grew up in extreme eastern New Mexico is my main authority on scaled quail. From what he says they are damnably hard to get into the air, preferring to run rather than fly, even more than pheasants. Their general tactic is to start running far ahead of a dog or hunter, along a wash or coulee where the grass or brush is higher (in this they sound much like sage grouse in hot weather) and then, if they feel like it, flushing way out of range. My authority says that dogs can be a help, if only to chase the birds and make them fly (mostly out of range), but at least this convinces you that they can fly and aren't miniature ostriches.

Probably the best method of hunting scaled quail, if you're a bobwhite hunter or otherwise bound by convention, is to start chasing the little beggars the moment you see them. Charles Waterman, an outdoor writer as honest and knowledgeable as any, says that a gradually gaining runner has a better chance of getting the birds up in range, because a quick pursuit can cause an immediate, wild flush. He also says that often nothing works, except strong language to relieve the soul.

The farther southwest you travel in the grasslands, the less grass and more cactus you're liable to run into, so good sturdy boots and a cactus-wise dog are advisable. Otherwise you'll be picking stickers out of both yourself and the dog all day long, perhaps more enjoyable than the actual hunting.

Indications are that many hunters cannot control their baser instincts when hunting scaled quail and actually shoot them on the ground. My cousin-in-law notes that he always had his best success when he "got a whole bunch of 'em huddled together in one spot." With that we'll leave the scaled quail and go on to better subjects.

Where to Go

Colorado and South Dakota are not thought of as quail states, but they offer surprisingly good hunting in restricted areas during mild years. South Dakota's quail are found in the four or five extreme southeastern counties, along the Missouri River, while Colorado's are most heavily harvested between Denver and Sterling, an indication that there are either lots of hunters or lots of quail around Denver. Probably the former. Quail are also common throughout eastern Colorado, but the hunting pressure might be less elsewhere.

Iowa's quail are found along the edges of the central grasslands, but it isn't exceptional hunting, being too far north. Nebraska's bobwhite are generally plentiful throughout the eastern third of the state, and best in the southeast.

Oklahoma and Kansas are the heart of the prairie bobwhite country, offering hunting as good as anywhere else on the continent. Oklahoma's hunting is best in the central and western parts of the state, with a few good areas in the cleared portions of the southwest. Kansas quail are abundant in the eastern third of the state, good in the middle and only fair in the west, though certain local areas can produce good hunting anywhere in the state. Texas and New Mexico also offer bobwhite hunting, with New Mexico's birds being poorly distributed along the eastern border. Almost all of Texas is bobwhite country, except for the extreme western part, but the plains hunting is found in the Panhandle, whose northeast corner offers hunting about as good as Oklahoma's.

Bobwhites, unbeknownst to most hunters, also inhabit eastern Washington, Oregon's Willamette Valley, and the Oregon-Idaho border region.

Scaled quail are more a southwestern bird. Their heaviest populations are in New Mexico (throughout the state) and the Texas Panhandle. Seasons are also held in southeastern Colorado, southwest Kansas, and southwestern and Panhandle Oklahoma. The farther northeast from New Mexico you travel the fewer scaled quail and the more bobwhites you find.

Merriam's turkeys have been transplanted into a great deal of northern plains habitat, and now provide hunting from the Canadian border down into Texas, along with the Rio Grande subspecies. This band is in typical northern turkey habitat: semi-open ponderosa pine forest.

Chapter Eleven:
Wild Turkey

(Melagris gallopavo)

It was opening day of the Montana deer season, and I'd made a promise to guide my brother-in-law, who'd never hunted deer before, in the country above the Tongue River, in southwestern Montana. I'd never hunted the country myself, but some friends had hunted turkeys there earlier and reported they'd almost been trampled by mule deer. After a reconnoiter run the day before the season opened, we drove in the gray light of early plains dawn across 60 miles of gravel to our appointed place.

I'd never hunted turkeys, or so much as seen a wild one, but Montana has a fall turkey season running with the deer season. Either gobblers or hens were legal, and rifles fair, so I'd bought a two-dollar turkey tag in Miles City just in case we stubbed our toes on a turkey.

We'd timed our departure just right, and as the gray haze of dawn left the pine-topped hills, we were walking along just below a ridge-top. We'd seen about a dozen deer along the roads during the drive to our chosen area under Liscomb Butte, and I anticipated no trouble in finding a deer for Skip, especially since Montana at that time allowed either-sex hunting. A mule deer doe is usually an easy target on opening day, and Skip was more interested in venison than antlers.

We skulked along for perhaps five minutes, stopping now and then to glass the canyon below us and the hill opposite. It was still half-dawn when I spotted movement across the canyon, directly opposite and little below our elevation.

"What's that?" I whispered. Skip shrugged. He was beginning to look bored. He'd worked overtime the day before and perhaps he wanted to go home and get some rest.

Then a sound came to us on the air, something between a dying rabbit and squeaking styrofoam. I cocked my head toward the sound, listening, and caught it better the second time.

"That's a turkey!" I said. Skip's eyes opened a little bit. "A hen turkey!" I'd never heard even a tame hen turkey before, but something, perhap's hunter's instinct and *Sports Afield*, assured me that it was indeed a hen turkey.

I glassed the opposite hill again. There! Yes, I saw them, like a crowd of porcupines, slow-moving and grayish black in the half-light, distant across the canyon. There were perhaps eight or ten, moving along deliberately, heading toward a patch of trees. I looked desperately around — there was no way we could circle above them before they'd get into the trees.

"Gimme that rifle!" Skip had my .243, which I'd filled with slightly underloaded handloads just in case we ran into a feathered deer. He handed it to me, and I looked around for a rest. The slope was about 30 degrees, and I couldn't even lean against any of the trees. Finally I wrapped my arm in the sling, cranked the scope up to 9x, sat down with my heels in the layer of pine needles, held just above the back of one of the black dots and squeezed the trigger. The whole flock made an ungodly noise and scattered downhill a little ways, then stopped and craned their necks, unable to tell who or what was shooting at them.

Not that far, I thought to myself, realizing they were closer than I'd estimated, just seeming far away in the dim light. I held just below the back line of the nearest bird; at the second shot the main flock took off, running for the timber, but my bird fluttered perhaps 30 feet the other direction and disappeared behind a small bush.

Ten minutes later, chest heaving from running downhill and up the other side, I hefted a ten-pound hen. At that range, the loaded-down deer bullet had done little damage, and a month later the bird had its coming-out party on our Thanksgiving table.

92

Since then I've hunted western turkeys a few more times, and found that my long-range shot had been by no means extraordinary. Eastern turkey hunters are used to calling gobblers during the spring mating season and killing them at short range with shotguns. That can also be done in the spring in the West, but Western birds and hunters are unfettered by the traditions of turkey hunting, and almost anything can happen. Including, as we've seen, a neophyte hunter out to find someone else a deer shooting a turkey at 250 yards with his favorite jackrabbit rifle.

Most plains turkey areas are semi-open patches of timber, juniper and pine in the north, and cottonwood stands farther south, a cross between forest and grassland, what might be called open cover. Turkeys do amazingly well in the West, even on the northern plains of Montana and the Dakotas, if they have just enough cover to protect them from a bad winter and just enough open space to keep the snow blown away so they can feed. They thrive in the conifer-topped breaks along the Missouri River and in similar country in the foothills of the Black Hills. They're abundant in the cottonwood stands of Oklahoma and Texas, and in the thickets that trace the dry watercourses of parts of Nebraska.

There are often two turkey seasons in the West, a spring and fall, with the spring season being limited to gobblers and the fall season either-sex. I suspect that most of the turkeys taken during Montana's and other states' fall seasons are shot by deer hunters that happen across a flock, like my opening day experience. Most of the fall hunters after turkeys specifically, usually hunt them the way they do deer — still-hunting in the early morning and evening, even using binoculars to spot the birds. Sometimes a roosting area can be found, which is usually a tree or stand of trees, often in a small canyon or coulee. You can tell it's a roosting tree even if no turkeys are in it, because of gravity, which brings to earth all the normal by-products of a turkey's life. These look like large chicken droppings, and if you've never seen chicken droppings, you will recognize them anyway.

Once you've found a roost, you have several options. One is to try to sneak up on the roost in early morning and either try to shoot one of the turkeys out of the tree or scatter the flock, hoping to spot a bird as they try to re-gather. Shooting birds out of trees is considered poor form in some areas but I am not a traditional

93

turkey hunter. Usually it's easier to scatter the birds, producing easier shooting because it will be lighter as they try to regroup.

In good turkey country, it's often easy to locate the birds in early morning while they're out feeding. For one thing, they're often noisy, like those birds I heard near Liscomb Butte. Once the sun rises and they drift into cover, though, they're hard to find. Some hunters are successful during mid-day by hunting cover with a shotgun and shooting the birds on the wing. I've never attempted this feat, primarily because I consider a turkey more of a big game animal than little birds that you wingshoot, but that's my prejudice. I just get more enjoyment out of stalking and still-hunting.

Sometimes it's possible to drive turkeys like deer, and in many ways they act much like whitetails. A couple of hunters moving up a canyon can often drive a flock past another hunter, since turkeys, like most big game animals, prefer to retreat uphill. They can really move, too, even on the ground. A big gobbler legging it for cover can move a hell of a lot faster than a pheasant and prefers to travel that way when headed uphill. Going down, they fly.

Actually, during fall a deer hunter using deer-hunting methods will usually be able to get a shot at a turkey in country where rifle hunting is allowed. Where only shotguns are legal, finding a roosting area may be the most successful tactic, with driving and wingshooting coming in second. It's hard to give advice about how to hunt in different areas because turkeys, like pheasants and deer, can develop different habits in different terrain. I've seen a flock picking its way through sagebrush along the Tongue and have heard that the birds can also be found in sage down in Oklahoma and Texas. The only broad habits that you can be sure of are that turkeys will be on the roost until dawn, then feed until full light; be found in cover during the day, then feed again in late afternoon; find water somewhere during that time, and then roost at dusk.

Spring turkey hunting is another proposition altogether. Spring seasons are gobbler seasons, and even in states where rifles are legal in the fall, shotguns are the only spring firearms in most cases. Spring is the breeding season, the time when toms gobble and strut, fanning their tailfeathers in the classic Thanksgiving pose. The hunting procedure is to act like a hen turkey, calling a gobbler within range of the scattergun. I'm not really much of a turkey caller, but the gist of what most experts say is that calling is most effective early in the morning and late in the afternoon, and the less you call the better. The best way to learn to call turkeys is to listen to a real hen in the woods, which sounds unlike anything a female bird should sound like. A second way is to find someone who knows how to call turkeys and listen to him. There are many different kinds of turkey calls on the market, some of the newer ones being easier to use than the old cedar box and chalk slate, but not so fragrant.

The sound of a wild turkey gobbling is not the semi-funny sound most turkey neophytes imagine, but a truly wild sound, incredibly loud and booming, ranking right up there with elk bugling and coyotes howling as one of nature's best spine-tinglers. Some hunters listen for a gobble, then start their hen call; others use their calls to induce a gobble. If the gobbler is interested, he'll answer right away. As a matter of fact a really hot gobbler will answer just about anything. An owl hooting drives them nuts. One time I listened to an owl and a gobbler taunt each other for half-an-hour. I wonder what would have happened had they met.

In thick cover, the caller can get the turkey to come to him, but it's been my experience that in more-open turkey country it's often easier to go to the bird. In either case, it's a great help to be above the bird because of their uphill-walking tendency. Camouflage and stillness are absolutely necessary if you're trying to get a turkey to come to you, as turkeys, like most gamebirds, are not color blind. It must be camouflage that matches the surrounding vegetation closely. Camouflage is equally necessary to the hunter stalking a gobbling bird.

The hunter trying to call a bird sometimes has the disconcerting experience of having the bird come up behind him. This is an almost impossible situation for a hunter as by the time he whirls to shoot, the bird will often be out of range or behind a tree.

Going to a calling turkey is often necessary in semi-open country, as the birds have a tendency to sit out in clearings; it's especially appropriate in states where spring rifle hunting is legal. In much northern turkey country, this may be the only way you're going to get close to a bird, especially if the weather is warm.

I've taken all my turkeys with rifles, as Montana law allows them both in spring and fall. I usually use a .243, probably the most popular northern plains turkey gun, using handloads loaded way down in spring and not so far down (because of deer) in fall. There are solid-point (non-expanding) bullets available for reloading in both the .243 (6mm) and .22 calibers, and factory-loaded solids in some .22 centerfire calibers, like the .222 and .223 Remington. I used a solid .243 one year and had a bad experience with it. I shot a gobbler about 125 yards away, and just as I squeezed the trigger he stepped forward. I'm sure he was hit, probably somewhere just back of the wing-butts (the classic rifle shot placement on turkeys, and where I was holding), but we never found him, even with a dog. Even a loaded-down soft-point would have put him down right there. I know solids will kill turkeys with exact placement, but after losing a turkey with a shot I thought was easy, I don't use them anymore, at least in small calibers. Cast-bullet loads in calibers of .30 or over are effective, because of their flat point and larger diameter.

Soft-point loads must be loaded down if you are at all interested in saving turkey meat. The hen I shot with the .243 was taken with a handload using a 105-grain bullet at about 2700 feet per second muzzle velocity, and out past 200 yards it did little damage, just punching a pencil-sized hole through the breast going in and making a quarter-sized hole going out, with no bullet fragmentation. Even better is a velocity of 2400 feet per second or less. Perhaps the best factory-loaded turkey rifle is the .22 Hornet, which uses a 45-grain bullet at about 2700 feet per second; because of the small bullet, meat damage is minimal. The popular .222 is also usable, but its factory velocity of over 3000 feet per second means severe meat damage if bullet placement isn't exact. Handloaders prefer to load it down to Hornet levels when after turkey.

Actually any toughly-constructed deer bullet, even at normal velocity, can be used in turkey hunting if shot placement is good, albeit with more meat damage than a gun like the .22 Hornet would inflict. Some Montana turkey hunters that I know use the Winchester Silvertip bullet in their .270's for turkey hunting, though one guy noted that sometimes "it leaves more room for stuffing than normal."

The .22 Long Rifle is underpowered for turkey, and the .22 Magnum rimfire is marginal, especially with factory loads, which are either a solid-point that doesn't do any damage or a hollow-point that blows up. Some adventurous hunters replace the factory bullet in the Magnum round with custom bullets meant for handloading the Hornet and do all right. I don't know how safe this practice is, and don't recommend it.

Shotguns for turkeys are usually full-choked and hold as much shot as possible. From the shotgun hunters I've talked to I've had various reports, but the consensus is that smaller shot are best for the head shots usually taken at standing birds. Numbers 6 and 7½ seem to be the most popular in magnum 12 gauge loads. Flying or running birds need bigger shot as head shots are not practical, many hunters using one shell full of small shot for the first (presumably standing) shot and then loads of 4's or even 2's for followup (presumably running or flying) shots. Those few hunters who walk turkeys up and take them in the air use big shot. The resurgence of the 10 gauge has found its way into turkey-hunting ranks and many gobbler seekers are using 10's loaded with a couple of ounces of big shot, which will put a turkey down if anything will.

The best all-around turkey gun is a *drilling*, a combination rifle and shotgun using two shotgun barrels and a small-bore rifle barrel, probably a 12 gauge combined with a .22 Hornet. Since drillings are expensive and exceedingly rare in most hardware stores, we have to make do with the combination guns made in the old U.S.A., which have single shotgun and rifle barrels. These will do for the careful hunter (the kind that always remembers toilet paper in the field), but I'd rather have a second shot available in the shotgun. And even in the rifle.

Where to Go

Both the Merriams (northern) and Rio Grande (southern) subspecies of the wild turkey are available to the plains hunter, and are more widely distributed than they were before man and his instinct for trying new ideas (carp in America, agriculture, and democracy, for example) came onto the scene. Turkeys are found as far north as Montana now and provide fantastic Thanksgiving dinners for many lucky hunters who'd otherwise have to settle for the bland, plastic-embedded birds stacked like organic cannonballs in November supermarkets.

Montana's huntable turkey populations are found mostly in the southeastern part of the state, with the Custer National Forest south of Miles City being the top area in terms of harvest, probably because it's the biggest. Turkeys are also found in the Fort Peck Reservoir and Ekalaka areas.

South Dakota has good hunting for Merriams turkeys in the Black Hills, and Rio Grande birds have been introduced in the eastern and central counties, where they provide a limited (130 birds in '78) harvest. Nebraska's northwestern portion shares the Black Hills with South Dakota, and Nebraska also has turkeys along the Niobrara River, between Valentine and Merriam, in the northern part of the state.

Wyoming's turkey hunting is primarily found in the western Black Hills and in Sheridan and Johnson counties along the rivers, with some birds harvested in the Laramie Peak region. Colorado's plains turkey hunting is best along the eastern edge of the Rockies in the southern part of the state, in Las Animas and Pueblo counties. Texas has good hunting in the Panhandle (and indeed in all of the state except the extreme east). Oklahoma has outstanding turkey hunting in the western two-thirds of the state for the Rio Grande bird, while New Mexico has some birds along the eastern border, most being taken from the mountains further west.

Chapter Twelve:
Open-Country Dogs
For Upland Game

There are very few human beings that really understand our peculiar friend the dog, and I don't claim to be one of them. Oh, sure, everybody who's hunted with a dog or two acquires a vague semi-knowledge of what the inside of a dog's head does. But really understand them? Dogs, like the old Orient, are mostly inscrutable.

That's only fair, I guess, because very few dogs can figure out humans, either. It may be even harder for the dog, since theoretically he has fewer brains (though I'm sure some humans and most dogs would argue the point) and is forced to hang around with illogical, unpredictable, and often unskilled hunters.

Since I started hunting, I've really come to know only one dog, having had an acquaintance with several others. That one dog and I learned to hunt open-country birds together, and partly by accident and partly by design we learned each other's strengths and weaknesses. Neither one of us does everything right, but we do whatever we do together. He doesn't go off hunting by himself, a quarter mile ahead of me, because he's learned that he can't catch too many birds unless I shoot them first, something that some dogs never seem to figure out. He has a lot of virtues for

Though pointing dogs, like this German shorthair, do their best work on bobwhite quail, many open-country upland hunters use them with success on other birds, like pheasants.

open-country hunting, being light-footed and able to run all day if need be, unless the day is a little hot (in which case I give out early, too). He knows what good sharptail and Hun and pheasant cover looks like, something that's learned, not instinctive, though occasionally I have to search the edges for an entry way for him. He breaks shot, a trait that is usually called a fault in a black Labrador but one that is exceedingly useful when a rooster pheasant hits the ground with legs intact. Gillis is usually able and willing to plow into thick rosebushes for a tough retrieve, or bound across a coulee for a sharptail in the grass on the other side. He doesn't chase jackrabbits as much as he used to and has learned to leave cattle, skunks, porcupines, and cactus alone.

Gillis has a few faults, too, like most dogs and humans. Because he runs hard and hunts rapidly, he's apt to overrun a dead bird, especially on a warm day. He doesn't take hand signals well to his left, but that's really my fault. He's never learned, as a few dogs have, to head off a pheasant, though he loves to hunt them.

Most of us, however, never do end up with a perfect hunting dog, because most of us are not willing to put the time, money and effort into finding, training and otherwise dealing with first-class hunting dogs. Also, we don't use a separate dog for each kind of bird, and each open-country bird is slightly different from the others. If we want one all-around dog, we can't expect him to point quail like a statue and also boost pheasants into the air. It just doesn't work that way.

I'm partial to all-around dogs, though, and have done most of my prairie hunting with probably the two best upland all-around breeds: the Lab and the Brittany spaniel. The Lab's biggest virtues are in retrieving and in flushing moving birds, the Brittany's in pointing and in working tight, thorny cover, because of its longer coat. Individual dogs can obviously vary, however; I once knew a Utah Lab that pointed California quail to perfection when they waddled around his owner's yard, until the owner caught him at it and whaled him.

That always puzzled me. Field trial dogs are fine and a joy if they work well, but only if they have field trial owners. Most of us want a meat dog that works all birds reasonably well, and to do that you have to admit your dog's weaknesses and exploit his skills. A pointing Lab is as close to an all-around dog as you'll ever get!

101

Just what does a good open-country dog do? Well, it depends on the bird, but as a rule the bobwhite is the one bird best worked with a pointer. A classic bobwhite dog ranges far, points solidly and may or may not be required to retrieve. I've never trained a pointer, but have hunted with several, and it may be true that the classic bobwhite dog is "ruined" by hunting those other birds, which don't hold like the quail. If I were more of a purist, I'd say that two dogs might be best for all open-country hunting; a bobwhite dog, and another dog for everything else, from scaled quail to sage grouse, but since I'm not a purist, I'll just note that real bobwhite fanatics train and use their dogs for quail, period, and the rest of us make do with what we've got. I've never used Gillis on quail, but I suspect he'd find birds and let me know they were around soon enough for me to be prepared for the flush. And I know damned well he'd retrieve them. But all that would be heresy to a real quail hunter, so I'll leave them with their classic pointers and move on.

Pheasant are always the biggest problem for any dog, primarily because they run. Gillis handles them the way most flushing dogs do — chasing them hard to get them in the air. As I noted, some dogs learn that pheasants can be headed off and dogs like that are as valuable to a pheasant hunter as a field-trial pointer is to a bobwhite man. A good pheasant dog also does a good job of chasing down cripples, something that Gillis excels at, partly because he anticipates the bird's fall and is on the spot where it comes down. I once watched him almost make an over-the-shoulder catch on a falling ringneck. But he missed getting under the bird, and the pheasant took off running. It tried to hide in a small thicket, but the bird's tailfeathers gave away its position. Gillis dragged it out by the base of the tail and brought it to me. More than once I've seen him disappear after a pheasant into a rosebush tangle, returning several minutes later with the bird. Such retrieving techinque is invaluable with pheasants, and a plus with Huns and sharptails.

It also helps if a dog pays attention to what his hunter is doing in pheasant country, because hunting tactics can vary so much with the terrain. There's that patch of cover near Poplar that we work by driving the pheasants until they run out of brush — and then we stand and wait for any nervous birds to flush. Somehow Gillis has either learned or instinctively knows that if he pushes the birds, they'll run, so we both sit there quietly and wait for them to fly, when I shoot them and he retrieves them.

Huns also occasionally have a tendency to run when wounded, and they seem to put out less scent than pheasants. It helps if a Hun retriever is a little slower-working than the pheasant dog. Huns are so small that dead birds often hang up in brush well above the ground, distinctly puzzling to dogs used to working in two dimensions.

Both Huns and pheasants can be worked successfully by pointing dogs, but they (not to mention scaled quail) are restless birds, and any pointer man whose dog hasn't hunted either bird before may be in for some shocks. Actually the pointing dog that works best on these birds, and to a certain extent on sharptailed grouse, may best be called a "semi-pointer" — a dog that lacks iron staunchness and is willing to move up and point again if the bird moves. Some fast-working pointing dogs seem to have the skill of running right up on Huns and pheasants, pointing them quickly and seemingly paralyzing them for the short time required by the hunter to make the flush. Slow-working pointers have a hard time with both birds, especially with pheasant, because the birds hear them coming and wander off. Of course, the same holds true for a slow flushing dog, which is why many hunters prefer strong hard-working retrievers for pheasant, especially in the brush. The bird has to be convinced that if it doesn't fly, it's going to be run down, and a large fast dog is the best convincer.

There's another trait that both Huns and pheasants have, though in different kinds of habitat, that makes a dog that lets you know when he's onto birds a great help. Huns have a tendency to sit down in grass, often six-inch-high grass, especially after a flush or two. A pointer will let you know definitely when he's smelling birds, but some flushing dogs are noncommunicative. It's a help to know when a covey of Huns is near, at least for me, because you can be better prepared for the shot. Huns especially like to light in grass just over a hill, and when you come busting over, they swarm into the air and fly downhill. Pheasants will often sit in grass, and especially in corn stubble. Many a dogless hunter has walked past a rooster and had the bird go up behind him, offering a shot that only few people make consistently, especially when a jolt of adrenalin has been sent to the brain by the sudden cackle to the rear. A good dog will be hunting ahead of the hunter

103

Early-season upland hunting on the plains usually means that birds are in thick, shady brush, and many hunters prefer flushing and retrieving dogs like the Labrador. This Lab helped the author take three sharptailed grouse from the brush in the bottom of this Montana coulee.

and put those birds up before the hunter walks by.

Pheasants seem to be more likely to hold tight along the brushy edges of streams and ponds than anywhere else, so a pointer is in order for hunting around water, but in this situation, the birds usually flush over the water, and a retriever used to duck hunting is what you need.

Though the Hun and pheasant are the real runners of the upland world, sharptail, sage grouse, and prairie chicken can also give a pointing dog hell. Actually, when the sage grouse decide they'd rather walk than fly, they start doing so a long ways ahead of hunter and dog; unless your dog is adept at circling a mile or so ahead and working back toward you along a sagey draw, there's not much hope. At other times, the grouse hold remarkably well, and there's no real need for a retriever in most sage grouse country, as the birds don't fall into rose thickets and are good sized (easily spotted by even myopic hunters).

Sharptail and prairie chicken can be runners, too, or flush wild, especially in sparse cover. They hold best in thick grass or brush, places where a flushing dog is often needed to get the birds into the air. In stubble fields they get nervous when a dog comes bounding up. I once hunted a wheatfield with a man who'd just made a couple of trips to Oklahoma after quail. He thought the pointers being worked by the men he had hunted with were mighty stylish, so he bought a young pointer. That dog turned in a fine performance that morning — or at least he would have, if he'd been hunting quail. He worked one side of the field, casting wide and fast 100 yards ahead of his master, while Gillis and another Lab hunted my side, perhaps 30 yards out, a little slower. The pointer made a couple of stylish points, and held them at least until the birds went up in front of him, perhaps half a second. He might have worked out after all if he hadn't had an accident with a porcupine about 9 o'clock.

If this is beginning to seem like I'm down-grading pointing dogs for open-country upland game...well, to a certain extent I am. The problem is not in the dogs, but more in their masters. People who buy pointers are either the rare knowledgeable sportsmen who really know what they want and can expect, or the rest of us who expect too much from too little. For us, the practical, adaptable flushing dog is usually the better choice, especially on birds that don't hold tight. In most kinds of open-country upland hunting, too, the hunter has about as much to do with finding the birds as the dog. With the exception of quail, he probably has more to do with locating game. Usually the hunter picks the cover and directs the dog in whatever style is best. Even in vast stubblefields there are certain areas where birds are likely to be, and an open-country dog's best work is in locating birds within small areas, such as a dip in a stubblefield or a long patch of coulee brush; a wide-ranging dog, like the traditional quail dog, isn't needed or even desirable. Perhaps the other bird most effectively worked by a country-covering dog is the sage grouse, but most sage grouse country is so vast that even a pack of good quail dogs couldn't find a covey of sage hens.

Something to consider when working a dog on the plains is that the weather is often hot and dry, especially early in the fall. The hot-dry weather requires a lot of water both for hunter and dog. I've hunted a few times with characters who didn't bring water for the dogs and rarely hunt with those people again. If I do, I bring water myself, though you'd be surprised at the number of hunters who are offended by someone else's taking care of their dog.

Birds like Huns and sharptail are in thick, hard-to-work cover when the weather is hot, so dogs hunting early in the year need to be in good condition, have enough water, and shouldn't be worked too hard. Gillis once collapsed in a rose thicket, refusing to give up on a hard Hun retrieve — and he hadn't been out long, either. Ever since, I've been careful about heat. Most plains and prairie land is also farm and ranch country, full of springs, stock dams, and creeks, and if the weather's really hot, I've found that Gillis' day is made easier and longer by a dip in the old waterhole every hour or two.

Most hunters, even with good dogs, lose a few birds in hot weather because heat and dust dry out the mucous lining of a dog's nose, vastly reducing his scenting capacity. Warm, dry weather also reduces the amount of scent in the air. For this reason, I'm usually more careful about the shots I take early in the year, especially on pheasant.

Wind helps to dissipate scent quickly, especially in open grassland, something that is more critical late in the fall, when windy weather is common. It helps if a hunter has some bird sense; if his dog can't pick up the scent of a wounded bird within five minutes or so, it is certain the wind has thinned the scent and the hunter

106

should try directing the dog. Most dogs will hunt better without your interference, but being able to recognize when he needs a bit of help saves an occasional cripple.

Dogs are highly individualistic animals, and I hope what I've written isn't taken as some sort of sermon. Obviously I prefer flushing dogs over pointing dogs for most open-country hunting, but that's a personal preference, partly stemming from the fact that the flushing dog I've used for the past half-dozen years has done exceptionally well for me. It all depends on the dog — an excellent flushing dog obviously would be better than a mediocre pointer, and vice versa. The most important point, whether you raise and train a dog yourself (usually results in less than perfection, unless you are a professional) or buy a fully trained pedigreed hunter, is to learn the dog's strengths and weaknesses and learn to hunt with him and not against him. (The dog should also eventually learn to hunt with you; dogs that don't are worse than useless. I know — I've hunted with far too many such animals, which were always the canine apples of their various owners' eyes.) Even fully-trained, expensive dogs sometimes don't work with some kinds of owners and on certain kinds of birds. Most hunters who aren't professionals count themselves lucky if they own and hunt with one or two exceptional dogs in a lifetime. Most of us, if we'd admit it, put up with animals a lot like us: with many faults and a few virtues, but with winning personalities. In spite of a dog's weaknesses, I'd never hunt upland birds again without a dog. It's especially gratifying to hunt with a dog as a part of a duet, in which each realizes what and why the other is doing what he is. From a purely practical standpoint, even a half-trained mongrel will help most hunters find game, but it is that realm beyond practicality, where dogs and men still find themselves in a strange, prehistoric partnership, that draws most of us to hunting dogs. And makes us love them in spite of their faults.

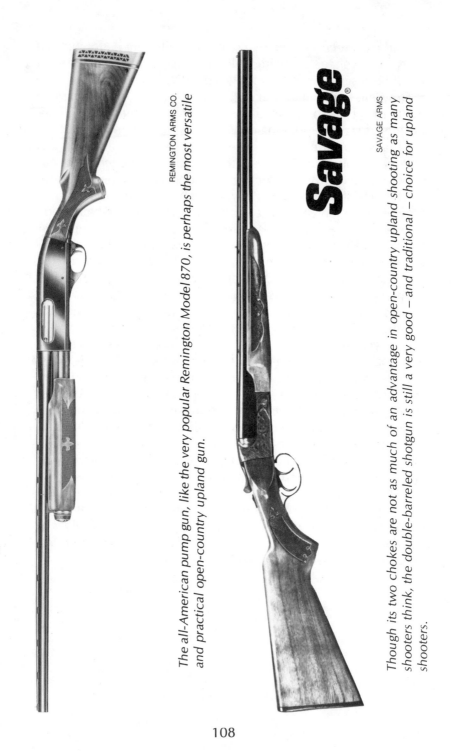

The all-American pump gun, like the very popular Remington Model 870, is perhaps the most versatile and practical open-country upland gun.

Though its two chokes are not as much of an advantage in open-country upland shooting as many shooters think, the double-barreled shotgun is still a very good – and traditional – choice for upland shooters.

Chapter Thirteen:
Open-Country Shotguns
and Shooting

It was a few days into the Montana upland bird season, the equinoctial end of September, and the coulees were filled with red- and yellow-leaved brush running light bright rivers toward the valley below. The day was warm, perhaps in the mid-70's, and we were hunting a large ranch in southwestern Montana known for its sharptail shooting. I was carrying a 20 gauge pump that had been modified by sawing off the barrel to 23 inches, leaving no choke at all. I'd used it on upland game, from ruffed grouse in willows and aspens to pheasant in buffaloberry, and indeed had just used it for the first time that year the weekend before, taking a five-bird limit of sharptails near my home in Poplar. It had been ideal for that work, the grouse flushing at ranges from 10 to perhaps 25 yards out of thick brush, the heat holding them tight to the shade. I now expected to have similar success 200 miles farther south. After all, the birds were again sharptails, and the weather was warm. Everyone expected classic upland shooting, with the dogs putting birds out right in front of the guns.

But the sharptails didn't know their own habits and were flushing wild. The stubble fields above the ranch house held covey after covey that took off a quarter of a mile from the nearest gun, and when we ventured down into a grassy, wide coulee below the biggest field, the birds still wouldn't hold. The closest shot offered all morning was perhaps 40 yards, too far for a cylinder-bored 20 gauge, even with a three-inch load. Instead of taking the limit inside two hours, as I had near Poplar, I think I managed to take three birds in two days.

The experience illustrated two things: I was an idiot to assume that all grouse everywhere would act alike and even when you hunt the same bird there's no such thing as an all-around open-country shotgun.

I'd have been smart that trip if I'd taken at least a couple of guns. A perfectly good full-choked 12-gauge pump was resting back in the gun cabinet in Poplar, but I was so enamored with the little 20 — which weighed around six pounds as opposed to the 12's seven-and-a-half — that I felt sure the 20 would do. It didn't.

If I had to pick an all-around open-country shotgun, there wouldn't be much choice. It would be a 12 gauge repeater, semi-auto or pump, equipped with a means of changing chokes, preferably several barrels, but I could get by with a variable choke or screw-in choke tubes. I'd be all set, theoretically, for anything from bobwhites in Kansas to sage grouse in Wyoming to pheasants in South Dakota.

I'll also say right now that since I don't have anyone looking over my shoulder (except my wife and my budget) telling me how many shotguns I can own, I just don't have one all-around shotgun. No, I don't own two dozen, but I definitely think the upland shooter can do better with at least two, or even three, firearms rather than one all-around gun.

Though the list of shotgun gauges and actions is as long as a political speech, selection can be simplified. There are really only two gauges that the open-country upland hunter need concern himself with: the 12 and the 20. As I type these words, I hear, off in the powder-hazed distance, eerie wails and accusations of heresy from all lovers of the .410, 28, and 16, and to them I apologize, but anyone who's shooting one of those guns already knows what he wants. I address the beginner or perhaps the one-gun hunter who's looking for something to complement his single, all-around gun.

Both the 12 and 20 are available in the whole range of actions, and both come in standard (2¾") and magnum (3") length chambers. What differentiates the two, and may make a difference as to which you choose for certain jobs, is the amount of shot each shoots. I'll also point out that the magnum-chambered guns in either gauge will also use the "short' shells, but the reverse is not true. *Ipso facto*, a magnum shotgun is more versatile than the short-chambered gun, although this idea has limitations — and versatility, as the man said when he entered the plow horse in the Kentucky Derby, can merely mean mediocrity. The short 20 shell is commonly loaded with ⅞, 1, and 1⅛ ounces of shot; the 3-inch 12 with 1⅝ and 1⅞ ounces. What these numbers mean, in essence, is that with more shot you can shoot farther, occasionally desirable in open-country shooting. It's like trying to splatter a sheet drying on the clothesline with a handful of juicy overripe chokecherries. You're going to be able to dot that sheet with purple from twice as far away if you can somehow toss a double-handful of chokecherries, a further advantage being that you won't generate as much risk of being caught. With shotguns the same principle holds: with more shot you can shoot birds farther away.

Keeping shot charges in mind, it's easy even for someone with the brains of a young cabbage to see that the 12 gauge shoots farther than the 20. It's also evident that since the 12 will handle loads from 1 to 1⅞ ounces, it is much more versatile than the 20, with its loads of ⅞ to 1¼ ounces. Here, however, we run smack into the conflicting Law of Avoirdupois. Most 12 gauge shotguns chambered for the 3-inch shell are heavy, weighing in at about eight pounds on the average, mostly to slow down the demoralizing recoil. A short-chambered 12 will weigh ½ to 1 pound less, and a 20 gauge, even in magnum chambering, even less. Most 20's on the market will come in at around seven pounds or under, many weighing 6-6½ pounds.

Add the fact that shooting quail with a 3" 12 gauge is like dumping a load of gravel on a cockroach — superfluous, wasteful and idiotic — and you begin to see the light. There's always a trade-off in shotgun shooting, one between weight of the firearm and the possible shot load. I've actually never seen much need, either, for the 3" 12 gauge load on upland game, though it might do something to tough late-season pheasants that a "short magnum" load of 1½ ounces might not. On most birds the standard 12 load of 1¼ ounces of shot will do all any one of us can ask.

I've made up my mind — as have a great many other hunters —

that the 3" 20 gauge is the queen, the king, and the Big Mac of upland shotgun chamberings. The standard 12 is better in some situations; enough so, in fact, that for the last ten years I haven't been without at least one of each. Strange to say, if I could just have one gun, it would definitely be a 12; but since I've owned both, I've hunted far more with the 20. The reason is that while the 12 is more versatile, the 20 handles most options better. The 3" 20 gauge load will kill sharptailed grouse and even pheasant cleanly out to 45 or even 50 yards, which is about as far as any hunter can consistently hit anything. The 1½ ounce 12 gauge load will add another five yards or so to that range, or possibly kill pheasants more cleanly, but for most shooting, neither of these requirements is needed. Since the 20 is usually a full pound lighter in the same model, for quicker shooting and less exhausting walking, most of the time it's my first choice.

Actions

Like the assortment of gauges and loads, action choice can be pared down considerably. Reliable, reasonably-priced guns can be had in break-action single shot, bolt action, pump, semi-auto, and either over-under or side-by-side double, but the only three realistic choices for the serious hunter are the pump, semi-auto and double. Each has advantages and disadvantages. First, let's look at the all-American pump (slide or trombone, as some people prefer, the kind who insist American buffalo be called bison, as if we're going to confuse them with all the Cape buffalo running around our national forests). This is perhaps the best all-around firearm for the upland shooter who wants just one or two guns. It's cheap, rugged, quick-shooting, and it holds more shells than a double. You can still pick up used or even low-priced new pumps for under a hundred bucks, and they'll last longer than any ten cars you'll ever own. They'll function under conditions that would make a pig flinch. They'll shoot rapidly — just as fast, for most of us, as a semi-auto — and will hold up to six shells. I may seem to be advocating firepower over skill, but I've seen too many "deceased" pheasants run off from their dinner appointment. There are also between one and two million different models of pumps — well, a slight exaggeration — on the market, and you can certainly find the combination of choke, gauge, weight, safety, style, shine and hair color that you want.

The semi-auto is a pump that doesn't have to be pumped. By either diverting some of the gas created by the powder charge's ignition or by using the recoil of the firearm itself, a semi-auto will shoot every time you pull the trigger. Sometimes. They are occasionally more finicky than pumps; the recoil-operated models are just about as reliable, though reasonable care will keep any semi-auto shooting well. They have about the same feel and handling characteristics as pumps, and can be had in just about as many varieties, but they are more expensive, though the cheaper models wouldn't break a really determined paperboy. The gas-operated models de-emphasize recoil, spreading it out over a longer time-span, so instead of getting slapped, you get shoved. Less recoil is more pleasant for the waterfowl hunter shooting heavy loads — it's no fun in a morning's hunting to let loose a box or two of 12-gauge magnum duck loads from a light pump gun — and the gas-operated models are also slightly heavier than the recoil-operated guns, cutting down on "kick." The lightest semi-autos on the market, and some come in around 5½ pounds, are all recoil-operated.

The double gun comes in two configurations: side-by-side and over-under. The side-by-side is traditional and has been made longer (ever since some wizard with a "hand cannon" strapped two cannons together) but the over-under is more in vogue, at least in America. One type has little advantage over the other. Some people say the twin barrels of the side-by-side confuse them when shooting. I grew up with one, and it's never bothered me, but I have a good friend who's an excellent shot, who gets cross-eyed when he looks down the barrels of my side-by-side 20. The over-under must be "broken" further to load, a real disadvantage in a small closet but not anywhere else. Most of us shoot outdoors.

The side-by-side is usually cheaper these days, though you can spend more than your monthly salary on either model and still not get into the really high-priced guns. The theoretical advantage of the double over the pump and semi-auto is that you have an instant choice of chokes. I've been trying hard to avoid the whole subject of choke in this treatise, but find I now have to deal with it. Choke, for those who don't know, is the small constriction in the muzzle of a shotgun, resulting in a greater or lesser "spreading" of the shot charge as it leaves the muzzle. No choke and you get a hell of a spread, perhaps 30 inches at 20 yards. "Full" choke means the minimum spread possible, perhaps only 12-15 inches at 20 yards. Obviously, no choke, or "cylinder" bore, is good for short ranges, full choke for long ranges. There are other chokes in between, like "improved cylinder" or ¼ choke; and modified, or ½ choke. Suffice it to say that every bird, every shot, and every instant would be ideally handled by a certain degree of choke, but such nit-picking is impossible. We end up using "open" chokes for short ranges and "tighter" chokes for long ranges. Modified, or ½ choke, is supposed to be the all-around choke, and like most compromises it is just that: fair for almost everything, but outstanding for very little.

Doubles usually have two chokes, one in each barrel, theoretically offering a great advantage over single-barrel guns. Normally, a double's chokes are in combinations of improved-cylinder/modified or modified/full. In theory you scatter a covey of frightened grouse and shoot one bird at close range, using the more open barrel, and shoot another bird farther out (since they've flown a ways since the first shot), using the tighter barrel. The poor guy with the single barrel gun, using his modified choke, has to kill all his birds at medium range.

But somehow theory doesn't work in practice. I know, for instance, that I can kill more sharptails, under all shooting conditions, with a full-choked 12 gauge than I can with a double. Why? Sharptails are open-country birds. You don't have to shoot them quickly liked ruffed grouse. With a full-choked 12, I take most of my sharptails at between 30 and 40 yards, some out to 50. With a double I'm limited because I have one "open" barrel, and on days when the birds are flushing wild, they may be just on the edge of that barrel's range when they fly. Essentially my double has become a single-shot.

This may sound as though I'm down-grading the double in favor of the pump or semi-auto. In terms of purely practical shooting, I am. The lightest doubles and the lightest repeaters are about the same weight, but there is a balance difference, a double being "muzzle-light" compared with other guns, a help in quick pointing, but I don't know whether that's an advantage in open-country shooting. For me, the only real advantage that a double has over its more-mechanical brothers is its ability to handle the ugliest reloads in creation; also, if you have a gun equipped with simple extractors rather than ejectors, it doesn't flip the shells into the brush. This is important to many shooters, including me, whose incomes don't match that of the average junior-high Rockefeller.

What do I use when I go hunting the high plains? At least 75% of the time, a double. A double-barreled shotgun is a thing of beauty, balanced to perfection, proportioned like fine sculpture, mechanically dependable, and backed by the tradition of cen-turies, instead of the *nouveau shoote* 100 years or so of the pump and semi-auto. A double is refinement, simplicity and art. I know I'll kill fewer birds while carrying one, but not too many fewer, and since when is the number of birds killed the basis for a day's hunt? (On the side, I'll also save a few shells for future reloading.) If I desperately feel the need of a few sharptail dinners, or my wife says that a pheasant would be special for a Chinese meal she's planning, I carry the supremely practical pump. Otherwise, the archaic, impractical double is under my arm.

Chokes and Loads

Having already skimmed the subject of choke, I'll not mention it further, except to make some broad suggestions, with one qualification. No matter what is stamped on the barrel of your gun, or what load you use, its true performance can only be found through testing. There are all sorts of shotgun tests, from shooting at a tin can on a fence-post to shooting ten-shot "patterns" at 40 yards and averaging the percentage of shot that falls within a 30-inch circle for each of these shots.

Testing shows what your gun is capable of at a certain range with a certain combination of load and choke. The percentage of shot in a circle has some meaning. Cylinder barrels will usually put 25-35% of their load in that circle, improved cylinder 35-50%, modified 50-65% and full 65-80% — but those figures do not really tell what your gun will do on game until you've shot a large number of birds with various loads, knowing the percen-tage of each load. They also tell you nothing about the distribu-tion of shot within that circle. Was it evenly spaced or scattered in little clumps? Was there a mass of shot clustered around the center of the circle or was the shot spread fairly evenly from edge

115

to edge? The most meaningful test you can make is to stick a paper cutout of the bird you'll be hunting (life-size) on your target and see just how far away you can consistently kill that bird. Most "experts" say it takes four or five shot to consistently kill a bird. Shoot at a few bird targets from 15 to 50 yards out, seeing just what will happen — how evenly spaced the shot are and also where the center of the pattern hits. For most open-country shooting, including sharptailed grouse, pheasants, Hungarian partridge, sage grouse, and prairie chickens, you'll want maximum effectiveness at ranges from about 25 yards out to 40-45. None of these birds have to be shot at short range, so if your style is to shoot deliberately, you might look more closely at your gun's patterns at 35 yards on out.

The quicker shot will usually be better off with a more-open choke and the deliberate shot with a tight one. Under some conditions, even the cylinder bore is good for the above named birds. I have killed many sharptails, Huns, and pheasants with the sawed-off 20 mentioned at the beginning of this chapter. But such a gun is decidedly limited, as I found out on that trip to southeastern Montana, its maximum range being about 35 yards. Improved cylinder and modified are better choices for most shooters, the choice depending on which suits your shooting style and primary target better.

I've found full choke practical for northern prairie shooting, even of Hungarian partridge, but I also shoot more slowly than many hunters. The bobwhite needs an open-choked, light firearm, and the scaled quail, because of his tendency to run and flush wild, a tighter-choked arm.

Choke selection is also tied to shot size and to the weight of the shot charge. The most popular upland shot sizes are 8, 7½, 6 and 4, with 8 being preferred for quail and 6 for the larger game like sharptails. Occasionally, 4 is used on pheasants and sage grouse, especially in windy conditions or when the birds are flushing wild, but most of the time the popular 6 is entirely satisfactory. The mid-size shot, 7½, is neglected in factory loads, especially in 20 gauge. Many Hun enthusiasts, including myself, have found it ideal for partridge and some other open-country shooting, especially early-season sharptail.

Actually, the standard 12 gauge load or magnum 20 load of 1¼ ounces of 6 shot will do well on just about anything, except possibly quail, but many of us like to play around with other loads, trying to find the perfect Hun or sage grouse or sharptail load. It is important to use a shot size matched to both game and to the shot charge. Ben Burshia, for instance, used 4 shot in his 12 gauge pump for years, for everything from Huns to sage grouse, in 1¼ ounce loads. When he decided in his later years to buy a lighter gun to haul around the hills, he bought a .410. Using loads with half as much shot as the 12, he quickly found that the .410 is a poor sharptail gun, especially with the 4 shot he had so much faith in. Back to the chokecherries and the sheets: The less shot you throw, the fewer holes you'll put in anything. There is an old myth that a .410 will kill just as far as a 12 gauge if you are "right on" when you shoot. A surprising number of experienced hunters still believe in this myth — mostly because they don't test their guns. A lot of these hunters will tell you that a "real hunter" only shoots when he's shooting at game, and they'd never be caught in the same county with a patterning board. They just put down any long-range failures with the .410 by saying the hunter wasn't "on" when he shot.

Shot larger than 7½ doesn't work well in loads of an ounce and under. For loads of 1⅛ to 1¼ ounces, 7½, 6 and 5 all do fine, depending on the game you're after. A fine Hun load is 1¼ ounces of 7½; a switch to 6 is better for sharptail, and 5 may be better for pheasant. In 1½ ounce loads, nothing smaller than 5 makes sense. Try to balance the pattern's density with the shot's ability to penetrate game. The small 7½, being less ballistically efficient than larger shot, don't penetrate well past 35-40 yards, so there's little sense in loading more of them into a shell than will adequately "cover" a bird at that distance. Similarly there's little sense in putting ⅞ ounce of 4 into a 20 gauge shell; though 4 will kill out to 55 yards or so, ⅞ of an ounce just isn't enough of them to make hitting a bird at that range very sure.

Range and time of year will also dictate shot choice. Early in the season, when there are many young sharptails around, before the birds have developed their heavier late-fall feathers, an ounce of 7½ will do well on short-flushing birds. I prefer this load when the grouse are holding tight in the warm early-season weather, because it doesn't shatter bones as badly as larger shot, leaving a more palatable meal. But if for some reason the birds are flushing farther out, 6 will be better, and I always carry a box of 1¼ ounce

6 loads just in case. I use the lighter 7½ loads through mid-October in Montana, for sharptail and Huns, as pheasant season doesn't start until late October. Then I switch to heavier 6 loads for all shooting, sometimes going to 5 or even 4 as the season progresses and the birds get wilder.

Plastic shot cups have become almost universal over the past 15 years, so I won't go over their characteristics here. The latest shotshell upgrading has been the result of "hard" shot, either shot with a larger percentage of antimony (a hardening alloy) or copper-plated shot. The advantage to this shot is that it doesn't deform in its trip up the barrel and so more shot fly "straight" into the middle of your pattern. Not only will there be more shot in the pattern, there'll be fewer on the "fringe." These fringe shot have been badly deformed in the barrel; and often fly slower than mid-charge shot, and are apt to wound birds. With "hard" shot, the overall pattern is also more likely to be even, resulting not only in more and better-distributed shot in the center of the pattern than with normal loads, but also in only a few fringe shot. I've found these loads especially useful on pheasant. It's not so much that the birds caught in the full pattern fall quicker (there seems to be a small increase in solidly-hit birds) but that very few birds are "fringed," or hit by weak pellets on the edge of the pattern. There's more tendency to either hit or miss, with not as much in-between feather-dusting, which results in wounded pheasants. Of course, this would hold true with all birds, but pheasants are a particular problem when wounded. I can't recall losing more than half-a-dozen Huns or sharptails that I'd hit in any way over the past five season (using a dog, of course) but even with a dog a wounded pheasant in thick cover can escape easily. The one problem with such loads — and they're available from many factories as "premium" loads now — is that they cost more, less of a consideration to the reloader and of minimal importance to anyone interested in wounding fewer birds.

Open-Country Upland Shooting

Obviously, whether you are after both prairie chickens and bobwhites in Kansas or sage grouse and pheasants in eastern Montana, there's a tremendous range of both bird size and flight patterns existing in open-country upland shooting. But many of

118

the upland birds are remarkably similar in flushing and flying, and the same shooting techniques will work for these similar birds.

As a class, I'd lump the sharptail, prairie chicken, pheasant, sage grouse and Hungarian partridge together. The sharptail and prairie chicken are obviously similar, but the Hun and sage grouse? That's like saying Mutt and Jeff are really Tweedledum and Tweedledee. Let me explain. All these birds will usually hold tight early in the season or in warm weather and flush wildly later on in the year; all fly at about the same speed; and all take off as quickly as they can, flatten out, and then fly relatively straight. Psychological factors make us think that the Hun is hard to hit, that the pheasant is traveling faster, or that the sage hen would have a hard time winning a race against a fast tricycle.

Shots at all of these birds can usually be taken deliberately when the birds hold tight. A problem of hunting Huns in sharptail country is that the little birds seem to fly faster and get out of range much more quickly than sharptails. I usually miss badly on the first couple of Hun shots every year, and then, when the shooting is over and I realize they have flushed only 25 yards away instead of 40, I'm tempted to implore the nearest fencepost to kick me. Part of the problem with Huns is that they tend to hold in short grass — they're often not anywhere near where a respectable sharptail will be, such as in civilized brush which you can walk up to in a dignified manner and send your dog in for the flush. Oh, no — those damn Huns will sit down in the equivalent of an unmowed lawn and come up around your ankles like a bunch of bumblebees with hyperactive pituitaries.

In close-flushing sharptail and prairie chicken situations, the birds are often ridiculously easy to hit. Early in the season they'll often dive right back into another patch of brush after being rousted out of the first one, holding well for singles shooting. Many times I've put up a covey of sharptails and had the birds scatter in a long thin line down through a brushy coulee. There is no more enjoyable shooting — you just follow the brush, putting up single after single. Warm-weather sharptail are perhaps the easiest birds of all for the deliberate shotgun hunter — they don't flush as loudly as pheasant, seem to be slower than Huns, and are often predictable.

Pheasant are about the same size as sharptail, but less predictable, and a close flush would scare an angry grizzly bear. In addition, they're bright-colored, long (because of the tail), and tough, so it's not surprising they sometimes seem hard to collect. Often the tendency, in response to the loud, raucous flush, is to shoot too soon, then to make haste with the second shot and blow it, too. There is nothing I can really say except that they are not any harder to hit than sharptails. If you concentrate and treat them the same way, they'll fall down, too. I find myself doing better on them when I'm prepared for a flush than when they come up unannounced between my feet screaming like an injured eagle and flapping like animate B-52's. The main point is to hit them hard and hit them as often as they need to be hit, until they don't move. Some shooters do better when they remember to shoot at a pheasant's head and not his tail. Makes sense, since the tail contains few vital organs.

The sage hen is the opposite of the Hun, in a way. He is so big and apparently so slow that you forget that to hit a moving object you have to aim in front of it. Sage grouse also sometimes appear to be in range when they're not. I was riding along a ranch road with a ranch-hand friend of mine once, after a fruitless deer quest, when we came upon a sage grouse standing at the edge of the road. My friend, a typical Western native, saw his chance for some easy meat, leaning out the window, shotgun in hand, for a quick ground-sluicing. He shot, and the bird slowly took off, sailing down a long shallow coulee and followed by a dozen other grouse that had been in the sage by the road. I paced off the shot, finding that the bird had been about 80-90 yards away. Despite the optical illusion, however, close-flushed sage grouse are easy to hit and surprisingly easy to put down, too, for birds of their size. I've killed far more with 1¼ ounces of 6 shot than anything else and have never felt the slightest need for more power. I did knock down three once with 1½ ounce loads of 2 shot, but that was while I was sneaking through sage toward a bend in the Poplar River where 50 geese had been hanging out. When I saw a sage hen's head pop curiously up from behind some tall sage, I trusted the old adage about a bird in the hand and walked them up. There were a rooster and two hens, and the goose loads put them down like a semi squashes a Porshe. Just an excess of power.

The above comments, I remind you, all apply to early-season

birds, when heat, a surfeit of young, innocent birds of the year, and not much shooting combine to provide close flushes and easier, predictable shooting. Later on, it's another story. When sharptails get up at the edge of your range, there's a need to be both quick and deliberate, something that sounds mutually exclusive and often is. Wild sharptails on a cold, windy November day can be as tough a target as wild Huns on a cold, windy November day. Sometimes it's better to give up. Pheasant and sage grouse can be just as bad, or worse, because late season birds are the toughest. More shot, larger shot, and careful shooting are required on all these game birds when they become wild.

I prefer the "pointing out" or sustained lead method of shooting for all these birds. There are two basic styles of shotgun shooting, and the pointing out method implies nothing more than swinging the shotgun ahead of the bird, sustaining a constant "lead," and then pressing the trigger. I must confess that I consciously aim my shots when shooting like this, preferring a relatively long-barreled shotgun that shoots exactly where I aim it. Now, I know that many shotgun experts will say you never aim a shotgun, that you always "point" it, but I know that I do aim and do well in the process, as my shooting companions will tell you, once you knock them off the barstool and rough them up a bit. I like either a bead and shallow-notched receiver arrangement (actually a primitive set of iron sights, like a rifle's) or a full-length rib, that points exactly where the center of the pattern is going to be. In most shotgun theory, if the shotgun fits you right (supports your cheek correctly) and you hold it the same way every time, your eye acts as the rear sight. This is fine and dandy — if your shotgun fits you. I'd say that 98% of the shotguns used on upland game are factory stocked, for the "average" shooter, not for you or me. They may fit like custom stocks for perhaps 10% of the nation's shooters. Thus 10% of the country's factory stock owners plus the 2% who use custom stocks have firearms that fit them. This means that unless you have some other way of making a shotgun shoot where you want it to, you'll miss a lot. This is where shotgun sights come in. I can hear fits and snorts coming from the majority of shotgun experts, but the fact remains that "aiming" a shotgun, when the shooting is deliberate, is a common technique. Jack O'Connor, the late great gun writer, testified that Bill Weaver, the founder of the Weaver scope company, always used a 1x scoped shotgun on quail — which automatically implies aiming — and was one of the best shots O'Connor ever hunted with. I have a close friend who uses a "point-of-aim" sight — an optical sight with a single, red dot for an aiming point — on his 10 gauge goose gun, and he is the best goose shot I've ever seen.

All this doesn't mean that a stock that fits is not important. It is valuable in short-range, faster shooting, like bobwhite hunting. My short-range shotguns all have factory or custom stocks that fit me, and also open chokes. Just "pointing" a shotgun implies a certain amount of error, and an open choke helps allow for that error.

There are two ways to point-shoot — with a stationary gun or with the "swing-through" method. Stationary shots are usually taken at straightaway or slightly angling birds. In one case you shoot at the bird's tailfeathers; in the other, you hold slightly to one side and slap the trigger fast. For years the slightly angling bird was my worst shot because I couldn't learn to make it with a quick, stationary gun. I always tried to be too deliberate in my miniscule swing.

The swing-through method is best on short-range, crossing birds, at least for me, though many shooters use it on all birds. It involves swinging the shotgun rapidly from behind the bird in an effort to "wipe" the shotgun's muzzle through the bird's path. Some shooters fire as the muzzle covers the bird — the swing is so fast that by the time the brain tells the finger to press the trigger, and the finger does press the trigger, and the shot does get out of the barrel, some forward allowance is created. It works, too — other shooters use a little lead, shooting as the muzzle passes the bird's beak. It all depends on how fast you swing, your reaction time, the gun's lock time, and other factors. I use this method on sharptail and pheasant out to 35 yards, and it rarely fails me. Beyond that, I need the more-precise lead of the pointing-out method. Some shooters can't adjust to using both methods as the occasion demands, and are better on one type of game, like long-range sharptails, than they are on another, like quail.

I've completely avoided talking about how much lead is needed for different birds and different shots, because the lead differs so much from bird to situation to shooter. Some shooters, as I have noted, who use the swing-through method don't use any apparent lead. I'll usually lead birds about two feet (at least what appears to me to be two feet) between 30 and 40 yards, but that's obviously a narrow range. All you have to remember is to keep the muzzle swinging through the shot and either point or aim as carefully as the conditions warrant. Oh, yes, and appease the shooting gods by cursing (at least inwardly) when you miss and by acting, when you manage to hit a bird, as though you never miss.

JOHN BARSNESS

This happens even to the best of us occasionally. A sharptailed grouse goes out on the other side of a patch of brush, leaving Ben Burshia wondering what happened. The proper spot to be in is on the uphill side of the brush, where Ben usually is.

The prairies and plains are the greatest grain-producing region in North America, as well as the greatest waterfowl "factories". Combine the two and you get great hunting. Norm Strung took these three Canada geese from a pit blind dug in a plains riverbottom stubblefield.

MIGRATORY BIRDS

Chapter Fourteen:
Ducks and Geese

There was still light in the western sky when the two hunters stood below the edge of the dam, but they know this would be the last chance of the day. Legal shooting light was almost gone. Shotguns held tightly, the hunters hoped that the mallards had been feeding in the grainfields above the coulee that the dam spanned, and that the birds were "home" now, on the water, resting in the evening.

All day long the hunters had made little sneaks like this one, coming up below the small Dakota stock dams, first walking easily, nonchalantly through the brush and tall grass of the coulee bottoms, and then crouching, moving more slowly, sometimes having to detour the reeds growing thickly below the dams, fed by water that seeped through the earthen structures. Then there had been that last short rest before the final rush to the top, when the older hunter mouthed silently: *one, two three*, and they'd both risen, shotguns going quickly to their shoulders, hoping to find two or three or perhaps even a dozen mallards on the water, and then to shoot quickly, maybe twice, as the big birds pushed off the surface of the water, the hens quacking in alarm.

They stood below the dam's top, and a slight breeze brought the sound of mallards talking easily on the water. The hunters looked at each other, tensing slightly. The older hunter went through his pantomimed count, and as they stood in the evening air, they realized that all the empty and two-duck dams of the day had finally tipped the laws of chance in their favor. Two hundred near-silhouettes bobbed on the metallic gray water, but for a long moment nothing happened, nothing moved — not the hunters, not the ducks, not the air — and then the silence disappeared, suddenly swallowed by the sound of 200 mallards rising, squawking, flapping into the prairie sky. Two shotguns sounded, twice each, and one mallard fell with a splash on the water and three others on land.

Water — the key to all life, especially on the prairies and plains — is even more important to waterfowl than to other open-country birds. Not only is it the basis of their biological existence, but their home. And, like every other part of the wild grasslands, the pattern of open water — ponds, lakes, creeks and rivers — has been changed by man.

The northern plains, from eastern Montana and southern Alberta, all across the Dakotas and down through Nebraska, were a natural pothole region, dotted with small ponds and lakes created by the last ice age. These numerous little ponds, especially those of North Dakota and the southern prairie provinces, had been the continent's greatest duck factory, providing water and edge cover for nesting birds. When man entered the scene, he started to drain the potholes for more farmland. At the same time, he dammed many of the little coulees and creeks, creating miniature reservoirs. Later on he dammed the bigger streams, like the Missouri and the Platte, creating huge lakes, in some cases hundreds of miles long, where there had been nothing but moving threads of water before. Farther south, the state of Texas was much improved as a haven for waterfowl — that state had exactly one natural lake within its borders, but it now has hundreds of artificial impoundments, most providing some sort of waterfowl habitat.

The plains and prairies have changed, and the waterfowl have been affected as much as any other kind of game — sometimes for better, sometimes for worse. The potholes of North Dakota are still being drained in a short-sighted attempt to marginally increase grain production, and new reservoirs are being created every year to provide irrigation water, power, and "flood control" for the plains — incidentally creating more waterfowl habitat.

There are four main types of waterfowling across the plains, depending on the water or terrain hunted — small pond, stream, big lake, and field. Small-pond hunting is usually jump-shooting, like that just recounted, and is most common on the northern plains, especially in grazing country, where many dams have been built for livestock. Ponds, either natural or artificial, are prime spots for migrating puddle ducks, and a patch of water that holds nothing in the morning may be full of mallards, pintails, and teal in the evening. Most often the small dams of the northern plains are located in a coulee, sometimes between grainfields. Grainfield dams will hold birds longer than grazing-country dams, especially if the weather is favorable. A flock of mallards may stay in the same area for several days, feeding on waste grain. There's a wheat farm I know of in northeastern Montana that annually hosts a couple of hundred mallards or so on a series of four ponds, each several hundred yards "downstream" of the next. The ponds lie between huge wheatfields, and the ducks are so loath to leave the area that when jumped from one pond, they'll just fly down to the next and can sometimes be jumped at each of the four ponds.

Around small ponds there is usually some sort of cover through which the hunters can make a sneak. Artificial ponds are "naturally" designed for jumpshooting, the dam obviously being located on the downhill side of the pond, usually in a steep coulee. The dam itself is the cover — I've jumped many stock dams where the hunters didn't even have to stoop until just before stepping to the top of the dam.

Natural ponds are normally surrounded with reeds, which provide some cover but can be noisy. However, there are usually either deer or cattle trails beaten through the reeds to the water, and these provide quieter routes, especially to hunters familiar with a pond.

In any case, jump-shooting is a traveling experience. Local hunters usually have a route worked out, with perhaps a dozen dams and natural ponds along the way, that can be traveled in a

127

day or half-a-day. Each pond will have its own approach and character, and with a warm car and hot coffee between stops, jump-shooting is a comfortable way to hunt waterfowl.

Occasionally a hunter unused to jump-shooting (which is often the only way many local northern hunters have ever pursued waterfowl) will toss a decoy spread on one of these little waters. This can be an effective tactic, especially if the pond lies along a known migration route, like that between two larger bodies of water. Unless the pond is on totally private land, however, there is the distinct (and surprising) possibility of someone's jump-shooting the decoys. This will stop when the jumper realizes at the water's edge that he is pursuing bogus mallards, but until you've had the experience, it's sometimes hard to believe how many hunters really do take advantage of sitting ducks, even artificial ones.

The biggest difficulty in jump-shooting is in retreiving downed birds. Hip boots are usually inadequate, and even chest waders won't do the job on many of the silt-bottomed prairie ponds. A good retrieving dog is the best solution, but shore ice can make it difficult for even a dog to get a bird.

I was once hunting a series of Montana ponds with Ben Burshia. It was late November, and the first pond was ice-rimmed, the calm water in the reeds having frozen at night. I successfully stalked it, though, and knocked down a drake mallard, then walked back to the car to get the dogs. The two dogs could see the bird, but when they jumped into the thin ice they couldn't make any headway. I was wearing hip boots and figured I could break a trail through the ice to the open water. I was out in 30 inches of water, near the edge of the reeds, when Ben's dog, George, came splashing up behind me, eager to get at the duck. He tried to swim right up my back, and I ended up sunk to my chest in icy and rank marsh water. Since then I've been more circumspect about retrieving situations.

River hunting can also offer jump-shooting, especially along the sloughs and oxbows of meandering prairie rivers. Here local knowledge is an even bigger asset than in pond hunting, because the backwaters and bends that hold ducks are often hard to approach or even locate. Just following a river can produce ducks, but the hunter will often be seen before he's aware that there are birds ahead — a knowledge of good spots and how best to approach them is invaluable.

It might be supposed that since ducks, like fish, always face into the current, that an upstream approach would work best, the hunter coming up behind the birds. Well, it is the best way to hunt a river, but for a different reason. Anyone who's hunted ducks more than casually knows they can see almost straight backwards, because of their laterally-positioned eyes. Also, the spots ducks rest in on rivers are backwaters and other slow-current spots that either have minimal current or perhaps eddy against the flow of the main river, leaving the ducks looking right at an upstream-hunting waterfowler. The one good reason to hunt ducks upstream is that downed birds will float downstream past the hunter (and his dog, if he has one) obviating an often tiresome and fruitless chase after a duck floating away from the hunter. To chase a floating duck along a willowed riverbank, while I flounder along in chest waders, is not my idea of sport.

Many prairie rivers are shallow, sandy-bottomed streams with gentle currents, and even those over 100 feet wide are often wadable in the low water of fall. These are the best for jump-shooting, as even a man in waders can usually retrieve all his ducks, and the hunter with a good retriever should never lose any. The jump-shooter should avoid big rivers, like the Missouri, Platte and Arkansas unless he has a fine retriever, and even then there are times when not shooting is the wisest course of action.

The most enjoyable and effective way to hunt a larger prairie river is by boat, and the technique is also effective on small streams. The normal procedure is for two hunters to float a section of river, alternating controlling the boat with shooting. The best shooting results when the boat hugs the insides of bends, because the calm water is located there — and so are the ducks. Coming around the inside of a bend keeps the boat out of sight of any birds until the last moment; thick stands of willow that often root in the sandy soil deposited by the river on the inside of bends add concealment. Johnboats work well for this kind of hunting, their flat bottoms providing a stable shooting platform, but often require a small outboard to make headway upstream, often necessary when retrieving a shore-downed bird or chasing a cripple. Canoes are not as stable as johnboats, but are practical on smaller prairie streams and can be paddled quietly against the current if the need arises.

Another kind of river hunting popular in the agricultural river-bottoms is field hunting. The first hunting of this kind I ever engaged in was along the Yellowstone River, in southwestern Montana. The river along one stretch was closed to water-fowling for a period of several years and became a favorite stopover for Canada geese. The birds would rest in the river and its slow sloughs, feeding in the corn and small-grain fields that had just been harvested along the river. When I was working for a farmer in that area, during the harvest we deliberately left a stand of tall corn at one end of a field (baiting waterfowl by spreading loose feed on the ground is illegal, but leftover standing grain is not) and constructed blinds in the brush near the corn. Early in the morn-ing the big honkers would come in to feed — at least for the first couple of days. After we'd shot at them at time or two, they had to be left alone for a few days before they'd return. It was a most effective hunting method.

Other hunters in the area built pit blinds, using 55-gallon oil drums, in the middle of the stubblefields. Covered with brown canvas and surrounded by decoys, these blinds proved highly effective. Field hunting for snow and blue geese is also popular from Canada down through Texas.

Field hunting for mallards is *de rigeur* in the Canadian grain belt. The number of mallards that can be seen in a day during an Alberta or Saskatchewan hunt can't be imagined by south-of-the-border hunters. If you add to the great number of birds the fact that grain that far north is often yet-unharvested during waterfowl season and that many farmers are actually searching for hunters to shoot birds out of their crops, you have a hunter's version of duck heaven.

Big still-water hunting on plains reservoirs is perhaps the toughest hunting of all, but it can also result in large numbers of birds. Huge impoundments have been built on the plains from Fort Peck Reservoir in Montana on down to Lake Texoma on the Texas-Oklahoma border. These attract both diving and puddle ducks, as well as geese.

The biggest problem in hunting these areas is that the water is so vast that the best spots for waterfowling can be hard to pin-point. Guides are available on many of the bigger, more popular waterfowling lakes, especially on the southern plains, and are highly recommended to anyone hunting a big lake for the first time.

Though waterfowling is normally a sport taking place in windy, nasty weather, plains waterfowling can be windier and nastier than any. Larger shot, heavier loads, and bigger gauges are recommended for much open-country waterfowling, partly because of the wind and partly because of the open country itself. Shots are likely to be long, whether you're pass-shooting near a big southern reservoir, jump-shooting stock dams in North Dakota, or floating a meandering river. A standard 12 gauge or magnum 20, shooting 4, 5, or 6 shot in 1¼ ounce loads is about the minimum recommendation, and the 3-inch 12 gauge is even better. Geese, especially Canadas, need at least 2 shot in 1½ ounce loadings. Many hunters are going to the 10 gauge for geese because of the increased availability of guns and the upgrading of ammunition in that caliber, not to mention the necessity of using steel shot (which is less ballistically efficient than lead shot) in some areas, particularly on the southern impoundments. The big 10's are effective pass-shooting and decoy-shooting guns for geese, but are too heavy for most waterfowling.

Modified or even improved-modified are probably the best choke choices for most duck shooting. Full choke is at its best on a goose gun. Open chokes are sometimes handy for jump-shooting; my favorite 20 gauge double with its cylinder/modified combination does well on early mallards.

Many open-country waterfowlers like over-sized decoys. The open country means that birds can often spot decoys at long distances, and bigger blocks will sometimes call in birds that smaller decoys won't attract. Snow goose hunters commonly employ newspapers, diapers, or pieces of white plastic as decoys, making a 200-bird spread easy to haul out to a field, spread and pick up.

Where to Go

Waterfowling on the plains starts up north, with the fantastic hunting provided by the Canadian grain country. Saskatchewan hunters alone harvest 300,000-500,000 mallards a season along with 90,000-165,000 other ducks and 150,000-175,000 geese, over half of which are Canadas. The best hunting is in the southern third of the province, which is wheat country. Grain-country ducks are mostly mallards late in the season (when the best hunting occurs) as the pintails and most of the teal leave the country early.

Southern Alberta, south and east of Lesser Slave Lake to the U.S. and Saskatchewan borders, provides similar hunting, as does the southeastern corner of Manitoba. Geese include Canadas, whitefronts, snows, blues and Ross's. There are usually limits on the numbers of whitefronts and Canadas that may be included in the daily and possession limits in all three provinces, but overall limits are liberal, ranging from five to eight geese a day and seven to ten ducks, with possession limits double these amounts.

The shooting just south of the U.S. border isn't quite so spectacular, but late-season jump-shooting for mallards in both North Dakota and eastern Montana commonly turns up 100-bird flocks. The best hunting, again, is in the wheat regions: from Shelby east, and from the Missouri River north, in Montana; and in just about all of North Dakota. Hunting is also good for geese in this region, though North Dakota has curtailed its Canada goose season in the past year or two in a restoration effort. There are plenty of snows and blues in that state, however, and lots of Canadas in Montana, especially around the Bowdoin and Medicine Lake Refuges, Fort Peck Reservoir, and the Missouri and Yellowstone Rivers. The southern part of Montana is grazing country; most of the grain grown in that region and other Western grazing lands is found along the alluvial valleys, providing both rivers and feed for waterfowl, and the hunting can be excellent in those areas late in the year, when the ponds and lakes freeze.

South Dakota, Iowa and Nebraska also offer good waterfowling. I can remember one late November day, driving from eastern South Dakota south along the Iowa-Nebraska Missouri. Geese were migrating along the big river, and as far as I could see, big V's of several hundred birds each were high in the sky. For several hours I don't think there were less than 5,000 visible at any one time.

South Dakota for many years did not welcome out-of-state waterfowlers, only recently opening up the state to non-resident goose and duck hunters, a strange contrast to their open-arms attitude toward pheasant hunters. In almost all of the state, non-residents are still limited to 10 consecutive days of waterfowl hunting; only in the extreme southeast may they hunt all season. The Missouri and its big impoundments are best for geese and diving ducks; many parts of these reservoirs are refuges, so check carefully before hunting. The northwestern grazing portion of the state offers stock dam jump-shooting, and the northeastern part of the state has good shooting in the many small lakes that dot the region.

Nebraska's situation is similar, except there aren't as many big reservoirs. Jump-shooting is excellent in the Sand Hills region, with lake hunting better in the eastern part of the state, both because of the more numerous reservoirs in that region and because of the nearness of the Missouri.

Western Iowa also benefits from its proximity to the Missouri. Goose hunting is especially good along the big river, and corn-field mallard hunting is good in the northeast and north-central parts of the state.

Wyoming's and Colorado's plains have much better water-fowling than they did several decades ago, thanks to restoration programs and more water. The big reservoirs along Wyoming's North Platte River, the Bighorn River itself, and the grainfields near Yellowtail Reservoir, on the Bighorn, all provide good hunting, especially for geese near Yellowtail. There are also numerous stock dams in the northeastern part of the state and in the Torrington-Lusk area that provide good jump-shooting for ducks. Colorado's northeastern corner has many reservoirs, both mid-size and small, that provide good duck and goose hunting. The Lamar area on the Arkansas River is also good, and the grainfields in the Grand Junction area attract large numbers of birds. The best part of the state for geese is the southeastern portion.

The north-central and eastern parts of Kansas hold more reservoirs than the rest of the state, providing lots of big-water hunting. Glen Elder Reservoir (Waconda Lake) in the north-central area is especially good for ducks and geese. The wildlife refuges in the Great Bend area, farther south, provide good hunting for that region, while river-hunting and jump-shooting are the main attractions in the less-watered western portion of the state.

Oklahoma's waterfowling opportunities are excellent, especially for a state many hunters regard as dry. The grainfields in the central and western parts of the state attract significant numbers of birds, mostly Canada geese and mallards. The big reservoirs in the eastern part of the state provide outstanding hunting for ducks and especially geese, with snows, blues and Canadas available. The Arkansas River is good mallard water.

The plains portion of Texas provides limited waterfowling compared to the rest of the state, most Texas hunters forsaking the plains hunting and heading to the southeastern part of the state for the spectacular goose shooting around Houston. There is some good hunting, however, around Lake Meredith and along the Canadian River in the Panhandle.

New Mexico is a dry state, and the plains waterfowling is limited. Ute and Conchas Lakes, in the northeast, provide good waterfowling, and the Bitter Lake Wildlife Refuge, northeast of Roswell, attracts birds in numbers.

Chapter Fifteen:
Mourning Dove

(Zenaidura macroura)

Ben Burshia is not a stranger to hunting, having taken all sorts of big and small game in his long lifetime. As a matter of fact, he's probably had as much hunting experience as anyone alive in the United States today, so it seems strange that he and his wife Agnes (who has plucked, skinned and cooked just about anything edible on the Western plains) should consider me a fanatic hunter, far beyond the scope of normal nimrods.

"Why," Agnes will tell her friends, "John even shoots those little bitty doves." Ben's attitude is that "if you shoot doves, you might as well shoot meadowlarks."

Mourning doves bring out these feelings in people, especially people who live in the few Western states — like Montana — where dove hunting is not allowed. To many people, the little gray bird with the twisting flight and cooing voice is a songbird, not a gamebird.

What is strange about the whole situation is that Montana's neighboring state of Wyoming has long had a dove season, and the dove there is an avidly pursued bird. I lived in South Dakota the last year that state had a legal dove season, moving the next year to Wyoming, where I really learned to hunt and eat those tasty little gamebirds. If I could get Ben or Agnes to eat one, I think they might change their minds about dove hunting.

135

Doves are considered upland birds by many people, migratory birds by others. I guess they're both, since they prefer the upland habitat of most gallinaceous birds, but they "go south" in the fall, like ducks and geese. Since I've hunted them only in country where they're transients, I'm classifying them as migratory birds.

When doves come to the northern grain country, they arrive in countless numbers. September in northeastern Montana drives me crazy — doves are everywhere, especially near the bins where farmers have stored their grain. Eastern Montana and the neighboring Dakotas could provide some of the best dove hunting on the plains, if dove shooting were legal, because this bird loves wheat.

As a matter of fact, down on the southern plains, in Oklahoma and Texas, you can locate grainfields easily by the numbers of hunters waiting around for a shot at a dove. Dove hunting is a big tradition down there, almost more of a social event than an outdoor sport. Hunters surround the grainfields in large numbers, sometimes hunting with people they rarely see the rest of the year. And they shoot birds — tens of millions across the U.S. every year. A substantial percentage of those millions come from the grainfields of the plains. The wheatfields that stretch from Oklahoma to Texas north to southern Canada probably raise and attract as many birds as the rest of the country put together.

There really isn't much to hunting doves — it's mostly the shooting that attracts so many hunters. If you find a good grainfield, either surrounded by brushy cover or with some cover in its midst, and perhaps a waterhole nearby, you'll find doves.

The big group shoots are organized so that most of the perimeter of a field is covered, and any doves flying will offer a shot to some hunter. Farther north, the group shoot isn't traditional, and many hunters use other methods. On one ranch in northeastern Wyoming, some friends and I had good shooting at two little stock dams located about half-a-mile apart. Two of us would sit at one dam and two at the other. Since those dams were the only watering spots within a couple of miles, doves shot at by my companion and I would usually fly to the other dam, and sometimes back to ours again, after they'd been shot at there.

Waiting near a waterhole close to evening is a fine way for a single hunter to take doves. Camouflage clothing and some sort of blind may be helpful, but doves aren't as wary as ducks, and drab clothing and an inconspicuous stand are usually enough to keep you from startling birds. It helps to have a good water-retrieving dog when shooting around stock dams.

I've also had good dove shooting in northern areas by walking the edges of stubble-fields near cottonwood stands. Though doves will rest in just about any kind of cover (in Montana doves are always fluttering out of good sharptail brush, tempting the hunter mightily), they prefer tall brush and big trees, like cotton-woods. The riverbottom grainfields along the Bighorn River in north-central Wyoming are full of doves in September, and an evening's walk along the edges of the stubble usually has pro-duced at least half-a-dozen birds for me, often more. This shoot-ing should be tougher than it is because almost all the doves you'll shoot at will be aware of your presence, which means they'll start dipping and sliding in the air, presenting an irregular target, but somehow I have managed to down about half the birds I shot at. A good retriever is important, too, because doves can be hard to find in the thick undergrowth that often borders riverbot-tom wheatfields.

Doves are notoriously hard to hit, and if dove limits were like those of pheasant — two or three birds — I doubt if many people would ever really learn to be good dove shots. Fortunately for those who really like dove dinners, limits are normally around a dozen birds. A casual hunter is considered good if he downs one out of three birds; you're an excellent shot if you can consistently do better than 50%

There are two kinds of dove shooting, and each presents differ-ent problems. One develops when the bird is aware of the hunter, as in the jump-shooting encountered by a wheatfield walker, when a bird hasn't gotten up a full head of steam yet. The problem comes from the twists and turns the bird performs, often resulting in a twist when the hunter is turning. I do well in these cases for some reason, perhaps because I tend to ignore the smaller twists and concentrate on the main flight pattern on a bird. An open-choked gun, say improved-cylinder, really helps in this kind of shooting, but my favorite gun is a 20 gauge double choked cylinder and modified, an uncommon combination, but one I like. Jump-shooting doves in wheatfields is a situation when the two-choked gun can be used to advantage: the birds get up at varying ranges and aren't covey birds, so you usually are shooting at single birds. I like to use at least an ounce of 7½ shot, often more, because bottomlands in the north often harbor Hungarian partridge, but many shooters like 8 or even 9. Doves are small birds and easy to kill, so really big shot isn't needed. They'll also come down to fewer pellet hits than other birds.

In the other kind of shooting, the bird isn't aware of the hunter, at least before you miss him the first time. This essentially is pass-shooting, at doves flying either to feed or water. Often the birds will be high in the air, even directly overhead, and flying rapidly. Some people say that a dove can hit 60 miles an hour for a short time, and with a tailwind they certainly can. The fastest doves I've ever "clocked" were flying alongside my car on a Montana road at about 45 miles per hour. At any rate, they require an extra lead, especially when they're flying at a distance. For pass-shooting, doves I prefer a full-choked, long-barreled gun chambered at least for the 20 gauge magnum; the longer barrel is for a greater sighting radius and more precise pointing. There's nothing much to say about this shooting except that the birds must be led a long way; if you're missing, try leading them a bit more. Heavy loads of 7½ and 8 shot are best for this shooting, though some shooters use 6.

Like most hunters, I'm not a great dove shot; when my successes have come, they've been mostly the result of my picking my shots. Other dove shooters will try for any bird within range, and occasionally these hunters come down with severe cases of dove depression. The best cure for a really bad case of missed-dove blues is a lot of rest for the shooting shoulder, a bottle of good bourbon, and a pan full of sauteed doves.

Where to Go

Dove hunting is at its best from Kansas south, since most doves stay in those states year-round. Farther north they are migrants only, leaving Wyoming with the first September frosts.

Doves are ubiquitous, and although certain regions in each state may have higher overall concentrations, little pockets in less favorable areas may provide good hunting.

Wyoming's best hunting is in the eastern part of the state, Oklahoma's in the west, while the Las Cruces area in New Mexico and the central and Panhandle counties of Texas offer the best plains dove shooting in those states.

In Montana the birds take peculiar delight in perching on my backyard fence, one of their favorite areas.

Chapter Sixteen:
Other Migratory Birds

It happens at least once each fall, usually in late September or early October, when I'm out pursuing some sort of bird or beast. At first it will be almost subconscious, a vague hint on the edge of my hearing that tells me something strange is near, and then it slowly becomes clear — a faint, wispy flutelike warble, somewhere high in the prairie sky. I'll look up, searching, and then, higher than I ever expect them, will be the sandhill cranes, a faint undulant line curving and flowing as though over imaginary hills in the sky. That constant warble will permeate the air until they are gone, moving south.

It hasn't been until the past decade or so that lesser sandhill cranes have begun to receive serious attention from modern hunters, partly because of their low numbers for many years and partly because of their difficulty to hunt. More and more hunters are discovering, however, that the crane is a challenging and tasty gamebird, though sandhills are still far from topping the popularity list.

Part of the problem must be psychological. A Montana hunter I know had to assure his family that the bird gracing their table was a goose before they'd eat. They thought it was fine. Many people compare the crane to beef.

Cranes are big birds, averaging about 10 to 12 pounds as adults. Their color is brownish-gray, and they can sometimes be mistaken for great blue herons at long range, but not up close. They can never be mistaken for the rare whooping crane, to which they're related, since the whooper is white. Goose guns should be used for cranes, with full chokes and maximum loads of at least 2 shot.

The best hunting for cranes is probably found around Roswell, New Mexico, near one of the crane wintering grounds. Crane guides are available in the area. The birds can be decoyed, and are usually shot in fields as they come to feed; pass-shooting is also possible. When not on their summering or wintering grounds, they mostly just travel. I've rarely seen them alight in most of Montana; usually they put down only in waterfowl refuges.

Their summering grounds are in Canada, where the next-best hunting is found. Manitoba and Saskatchewan have limits of four birds a day and eight in possession, while New Mexico has a three-and-six limit. Canadian hunting seasons are held in September, just before the migration, while New Mexico's is November through January, after the birds have made the 50 to 60 day journey south.

Elsewhere the birds, as I noted, keep high and alight rarely, so the pickings are slimmer. Montana's hunting is fair, with a three-and-six bird limit, though not many hunters take advantage of it. The season is in October when the birds come through, and permits must be obtained from Fish, Wildlife and Parks Department offices. South Dakota also has a three-and-six limit, but with only 47 cranes harvested in 1977 — either no one hunts them or the hunting isn't that good. Wyoming also has a season, with 44 cranes being harvested in '74 and only eight a year later. Oklahoma and Colorado may be better bets; Colorado's harvest was 433 in 1977, though this figure may reflect the state's bigger hunting pressure. Oklahoma has good hunting in Jackson and Tillman Counties and near Washita National Wildlife Refuge, in Custer County.

Common, or Wilson's, snipe are also legal game throughout the plains, though they're largely ignored. Limits are generous, running from 10 daily and 20 in possession in Canada to the eight and 16 of most states. I've hunted them in eastern Montana, and though they're not the most exciting game bird, they are common in early October that far north and are tasty, though small. You need at least a limit for a meal. They are solitary birds, hard to flush, and found in the reedy areas near water. Wadered tromping through reeds will usually turn up a few, or a lot if you hit the migration just right; a good dog is needed to find them once they're down. In some water, boat or canoe hunting through reedy shallows can be productive.

Rails are also hunted on the southern plains. Oklahoma and New Mexico have a 25 bird limit, both daily and possession, and a few hunters hunt rail avidly. Both sora and Virginia rails can be hunted in the region, by the same methods snipe hunters use. Since both rails are tasty and challenging targets they deserve to be more popular.

Chapter Seventeen:
Small Game

The sky had just begun to suggest dawn as I climbed into a tree stand along the Montana Missouri. After settling against the bark of the cottonwood behind me and waiting in silence for perhaps five minutes, the forest started to perk up. I heard a rooster pheasant cackle somewhere in the distance, talking to the eastern light, and heard invisible feet slipping through the leaves: mice running under the three-inch forest carpet, like unseeable deer hooves as they ran, then stopped, then ran again.

It wasn't until the full light of early morning touched the riverbottom that I could see the shapes moving through the cottonwood branches to my left. At first I thought they were birds, but then some memory of my 12-year-old Minnesota autumn, when I'd gone squirrel hunting with an acquaintance of my father's in the hardwood stands between farm fields west of the Twin Cities, told me what they were. The forms were fox squirrels, big, two-pound red squirrels, leaping from branch to bole to branch, talking in the dawn. That morning I had a .270 in my hands, hoping for a whitetail buck to come slipping by, but the next time I visited this tree stand, I carried a scoped .22. I didn't tell many people I was hunting squirrels, because most Montanans would think I was crazy. There's just too much other big and feathered game around for them to mess with small game.

Desert cottontails can be hunted over much of the plains. This one was taken on a sagebrush flat near Rawlins, Wyoming.

144

Fox squirrels, to the surprise of many hunters, are common in the cottonwood-willow vegetation that follows the prairie rivers west into the Rockies, but they're largely ignored in most places west of the 100th meridian. Colorado was the only Rocky Mountain state which could supply me with harvest figures: 165 hunters took 1006 fox squirrels in 1977, all in the eastern plains third of the state.

Squirrels are so inconsequential in the Montana hunter's scheme that there's not even a season, limit, or license for them. Most hunters in the Big Sky state would be shocked at the notion of paying to hunt squirrels, as my friends in Minnesota and eastern South Dakota do every year.

This doesn't mean the hunting is poor in the Western states — far from it. In fact, it can be almost too good. Fox squirrels, even in the area around Minneapolis and St. Paul, where urbanites harrass them every fall, don't have the sagacity of gray squirrels, their cousins that don't range as far west. When fox squirrels are left alone, as in eastern Montana, they're pretty easy to collect. I wouldn't think of using a shotgun on Montana squirrels, as many eastern hunters do; there just isn't any challenge. A scoped .22 is more appropriate. I use solid-point ammo and try for head shots, but many hunters like to use hollow-points on the big fox squirrel because of the superior stopping power. I do recommend to new squirrel hunters a good big-bore scope on their .22, which will make dim-light aiming much easier than with the tiny .22 scopes. At least 6 shot is recommended for squirrel hunters who use shotguns.

Fox squirrels are found from Canada south to Texas along the western edge of the plains, but become more numerous (and hard-hunted) the farther east you go. I've never seen grays farther west than eastern South Dakota; they are popular game in the eastern halves of the mid-prairie states, from Oklahoma north through Minnesota and Manitoba. Shotguns are entirely appropriate for these hard-to-hunt little animals. When I was a Minnesota resident for a couple of years in my early teens, I'd listen to everything older hunters told me but rarely practice it. Most of them liked to find a likely place in the timber and sit if they were hunting alone, moving on every half-hour or so if nothing moved. Many liked to team up, taking turns walking and standing through the woods, perhaps 50 yards apart. The standing hunter would usually get the shot as a squirrel would spook at the moving hunter and run around to the opposite side of the tree. Grays are found down through eastern Oklahoma and Texas, and are usually found in slightly thicker timber than fox squirrels.

Rabbits and hares are also found throughout the plains. The most common are the various subspecies of the ubiquitous cottontail. In farming areas, rabbits are found in all the standard cottontail places: like woodpiles, the edges of fields, and brushy cover, but some cottontails live out in desert sagebrush. I've hunted desert cottontails around Rawlins, Wyoming, in midwinter, not exactly traditional cottontail sport. The best way to find desert rabbits is to hunt on cold, sunny days, driving along looking for rabbits sunning on hillsides, or to walk through little coulees and swales looking for rabbits under sagebrush, small trees, or wrecked cars (very common in south-central Wyoming). Other than their habitat, there's little difference between desert and "normal" cottontails.

There are also snowshoe hares on the northern plains, but coming on one just isn't predictable. They usually hang out in cottontail-like habitat, but I've jumped them up in badlands draws and other weird places, usually while out hunting something else.

Jackrabbits are classed as varmints by most people, because they're considered inedible by western natives. My father was one such native who grew up, he said, eating too damn many jackrabbits, on a central Montana homestead. The standard recipe he quoted was to boil a rock and a jackrabbit until you could stick a fork in the rock — the jackrabbit was then fit to eat. When I was 13, I shot a young jack, and unbeknownst to my father, my mother cooked it up in a stew. My father thought it was delicious but kept asking what kind of meat it was. When we finally told him, he went into the bathroom and relieved himself of dinner.

Even the older jacks aren't bad eating, though not as tasty as cottontails, or snowshoes. I've mostly hunted the biggest whitetailed variety, which ranges from eastern Montana and North Dakota north. These are a true northern mammal, turning white in winter. There are two main hunting methods: stalking with .22s (or even bows) and long-range shooting with centerfire varmint guns. Even a .243 leaves at least three-quarters of a six-to eight-pound jack intact, though not many people eat them. You walk or drive through a sagebrush flat, jumping the rabbits from their forms under sage clumps. The .22 hunter must be more circumspect. Rimfire hunting is more challenging in winter, when white snow and white rabbits blend, convincing the rabbits (actually hares for all you technical people) that they are better off sitting than running, at least for the moment. The hunter walks slowly across the sage flats, looking carefully for rabbits under the brush. Usually he sees the black eyes or dark-rimmed ears first. If the rabbit is too far away for a shot the hunter circles it in an ever-tightening spiral, until within range. Sometimes they can be approached to within 20 or 30 feet.

In fresh snow a spiral can also be used when tracking. Walk until you find a fresh track, then circle ahead 100 yards or so. If you cut across no track, start spiraling around the region from where you first met the track to where you circled ahead. The jackrabbit has to be in there somewhere, unless he has flown. If you do find a track on the initial circle just circle ahead again until you don't, then perform the spiral.

The whitetail jack's meat is more like pronghorn than rabbit meat, being dark and grainy. It isn't as sweet as pronghorn meat, however, but it's by no means unpalatable. The jackrabbits farther south, the blacktailed and antelope, are reported to be poor eating, but nobody I've found who asserts that has ever eaten one. Apparently the bad word is passed from generation to generation like a family curse or possibly freckles.

Because of the vast terrain and tendency for game to be found in isolated spots, vehicles are necessary for plains hunting. They have to be rugged, reliable and able to hold hunters, guns, dogs and – hopefully – game.

Chapter Eighteen:
Vehicles and Camping

Ben Burshia and I were hunting pheasants one late-season day, shortly after an unusually early blizzard had swept across the northern plains. We crossed a fallow field in my four-wheel drive, bumping over the frozen clods of earth to a shallow dry creek that angled near one corner of the field. There was only a skiff of snow on the open field itself, but the weeds and grass in the creekbottom had caught and held the wind-blown flakes, so when we came to the corner, we weren't surprised to find a level expanse of drifted snow. The rule of thumb when traveling in that country in winter is that if you can't see grass coming up through the snow, get out and check the depth before plowing through. I couldn't see grass, so I slipped the Bronco into neutral and hopped out to investigate. The snow's crust was hard enough for me to walk casually on, and I noticed what appeared to be a flat stone about three inches in diameter out ahead of me on the snow. Thinking that strange — after all, what would a rock be doing sitting on top of drifted snow? — I walked over and bent down to pick it up. As I did, I noticed the distinct cracks and circular pattern of wood. What at a distance appeared to be a rock was the tip-top of a fencepost. I was standing on four feet of hard-crusted snow.

I hate to consider what would have happened had I assumed the snow was no more than a foot or so deep and plowed on through. Well, I know what would have resulted, because I've seen people make that mistake. One guy had to dig all day to get his four-wheel-drive pickup out of a coulee. Some have to wait until spring.

It would seem to the unfamiliar that the prairies and plains are benign, flat hunting grounds, ideally constructed for vehicluar travel. However, most of the time you're hunting in the less-level parts, because few game animals live in the really flat places. And even in the level areas, there's a strange substance known as water that somehow disagrees with flatness, always trying to grow a valley here and a coulee there. Even a two-foot-deep washout can make life difficult for an unwary hunter.

Difficulties are compounded by the fact that vehicle hunting is the rule rather than the exception on the plains. Not that you actually ride around trying to spot game from the truck, and then leap out, gun in hand, toward some startled beast. Mainly a vehicle is used to get you near good areas, which sometimes are miles apart, and to haul big game back to civilization. There are indeed some game animals that can be spotted easily from a vehicle — pronghorn, for example — but the hunting or stalking is done (theoretically) on foot.

The need for vehicles in open-country hunting is obviously going to create problems in the future as fuel supplies get tighter, but more and more hunters are finding they can get by with a smaller vehicle than they have been used to. I've done a lot of hunting in mini-pickups, and unless the snow is exceptionally deep (which usually doesn't happen until most game seasons are closed) have found that I can, with some judgment, get most places I want to go. My present vehicle, a small four-wheel-drive, is even better, allowing me to get to the few places not reachable in a mini-pickup. More manufacturers are producing mini-pickup four-wheel-drives now, and these will probably become the hunting cars of the future.

Whatever kind of vehicle you drive, however, there are certain conditions natural (and some not so natural) to open-country terrain that the hunter should be aware of. Early-season hunting is usually the easiest in terms of getting around. The ground is dry, as are most seasonal watercourses, and even if you should get stuck, there's usually no problem in getting out (or walking out). There are a few problems to watch out for, however. One is green grass, which is found in some spots even during fall, usually in coulees and other steep places. Green grass is slippery, something a few people find out when they drive down into a coulee and then try to drive back out again. Green grass on a steep slope can actually be the difference between moving forward and sliding backward.

Dry grass can cause problems, too — not because it's likely to cause fires, though that is a possibility every hunter should be aware of — but because of the way it obstructs the driver's ground vision. I try to do as much of my traveling on roads (some admittedly nothing more than faint trails in grama grass) as possible, but there are occasions when off-road travel is necessary or desirable, and as long as the hunter takes reasonable care, this doesn't hurt dry prairie sod. (It is idiocy, however, to travel in a four-wheel-drive across the prairie after a two-day rain, tearing up some rancher's pasture. It doesn't do the sod any good, and does even less for landowner-hunter relations, which are bad enough already.)

At any rate, tall grass, say one to two feet high, can hide rocks, holes, tangles of barbed-wire, dead cows, and other distinctly unpleasant obstacles. A higher vehicle not only gives you more clearance over these travails, but gets your eyes up at a level where you can actually look down into the grass for rocks, lumber, and old foundations, difficult from a mini-pickup. Very wet years, with their abundant tall grass, can make off-road travel in lower vehicles a two-mile-per hour proposition.

Those damned watercourses also create problems — and they don't have to be big, either. One time I was riding with Ben in his mini-pickup, after sharptailed grouse on ranchland north of Poplar. We were driving a two-rut road in some badlands, just sort of drifting along in the late afternoon, when we came over a slight rise. Now there is an animal that lives on the prairie that loves nothing more than to follow rutted roads and make them more

151

rutted, and that animal is the domestic cow. Water erosion, on even slight slopes, aggravates the problem. The result, in our case, was that when we topped the little rise, the ruts of the road, which had been only two or three inches deep, suddenly became about a foot deep, slightly more than is healthy for a pickup with six inches of clearance. Making matters worse, Ben's reflexes jumped on the accelerator, as he tried to turn the pickup out of the ruts, when he should have jumped on the brake, which would have allowed us to back out. The ruts were a little too deep, however, so instead of driving out, we found ourselves spinning our rear tires over air, the differential hanging up on the high mid-ridge of the trail.

Fortunately, we had two of the most basic getting-unstuck tools with us: a shovel and a high-lift bumper jack. First we tried the easy way, to jack up the rear of the car until the rear wheels clear the ruts, and then push the jack over gently. Theoretically the rear wheels land to the side of the ruts. Unfortunately these ruts were a little too deep, and the jack became too unstable. So we jacked up the wheels one at a time and shoveled dirt under them and drove out.

Another time, we found ourselves hunting sage grouse across a vast sagebrush plain, continually having to cross the two- to three-foot twisted gashes that water tears in sandy sagebrush soil. With a shovel and a couple of three-foot-long two-by-eights we got across every washout, picking our spots carefully.

Actually, most dry-country "got stuck" situations can be handled with a shovel and jack. The high-lift jack is a marvelous machine: it can reach under bumpers that are almost touching the ground and can be used not only to lift three tons several feet in the air but to push and pull. With a stout chain one can even be used as a come-along if a big rock or small tree is handy. One time we tried to drive across a narrow, deep coulee that was slightly narrower than the pickup was long. The rear of the pickup hung up, the rear wheels spinning futiley above the ground. Five minutes later, after I'd stuck the jack horizontally against the side of the coulee and jacked the truck several inches up the other side, we drove away.

A shovel allows you to fill holes, primarily, like the ruts we got hung up in that one time, but the creative person (who is also, I must admit, creative at getting stuck) can find other uses for it.

Once, when a large, impolite rock sneakily found its way under our front end and situated itself so that we could neither back up or go forward without running over it again, I dug up some sod and placed it in front of the rear tire, right beside the rock. When the tire moved forward and over the sod, the rear axle went up and over the rock.

A bevel along the underside of a shovel makes cutting sot a whole lot easier. Dry sod can be as tough as carpet.

Another open-country hazard is water — often surprising you when it does occur, since it is relatively scarce over most of the plains. One fine fall day I was driving the edges of a field, hoping to obtain photos of game birds (most of which, by the way, are less spooked by a vehicle than by a man on foot). The field's edges, like many western fields that edge deep coulees and small valleys, rose and fell with shallow drainages that dropped into a nearby creekbottom. I was in the bottom of one such drainage when I spotted a mourning dove on a fencepost; I stopped the pickup and aimed my telephoto-equipped camera at the dove, which naturally flew just before I clicked the shutter. When I tried to drive away, I found that the dry-appearing ground was slick mud underneath the surface. I tried for an hour to get out of there, but since I didn't at that time have chains, a high-lift jack, or four-wheel drive, I eventually had to walk to the nearest road and hitch a ride home for help.

A rainstorm two or three days before a hunting trip should put you on your guard. Low and shady spots will be wet, often under a crust of dry-appearing soil. Creekbottoms can be another cause of distress. Many of the smaller prairie creeks are intermittent, and even if they run all year, there usually are a series of pools with narrow, shallow sections of running water between; often the water flows underground between pools, revealing nothing on the surface. Gravelly spots are safer; sandy areas are usually not firm and can even be quicksand, which slows down even a four-wheel-drive, though it is not the dangerous morass often portrayed in grade-B movies.

Large streams can sometimes be forded, usually at the traditional fords used by Indians and wagons. These spots are usually gravelly, too, and are well-marked by roads that disappear into the river and emerge on the other side. They're normally used most easily at the stream's low flow, which happily for hunters occurs in fall, during hunting season. They're handy when you know where they are, as bridges in farm country are not frequent; a good ford can save several miles of detour.

There are several types of soil endemic to the grasslands, each presenting certain problems to travel. Sandy soil is common, and loose sand can be miserable stuff to drive in, especially without four-wheel-drive. If you have to travel loose sand, it is best to get moving and keep moving, and if you start to spin, don't keep spinning until you're dug in to your axles.

Gumbo is another legendary western soil, a clayey type that is either rock-hard when dry or slick as axle grease when wet. When gumbo country becomes soaking wet, it is often best to stay out of it.

Later on in the hunting season snow can create problems, the biggest of which is drifting. Usually the really good blizzards don't hit until January, but occasionally a big snowfall is early, accompanied by winds. The biggest pitfalls are areas like the fence-corner encounter at the beginning of this chapter, where snow drifts into low spots. Wind will usually sweep the ridges free, but wind on deep snow creates a hard crust, which robs your vehicle of the power and momentum you need to plow through. Another entertaining phenomenon is the cattle trail that some-how always finds its way into the bottom of every coulee. You pull up to a drifted 20-foot-wide coulee and get out and poke the snow with a shovel handle to find out how deep it is. The snow isn't even badly crusted — fairly loose, and only a foot deep — so you back up and go roaring through, only to hit a foot-deep cattle trail hidden by the level snow. Guns, hunters, and anything else that isn't latched down hit the roof, and you're lucky if all you need is a front-end alignment.

Different terrain conditions imply different vehicle needs, and the biggest difference is tires. The most fashionable these days for four-wheel-drives are the big, wide, deep-lugged, white-lettered tires that give your vehicle that macho look. These, like fast-food franchises, suntans, and beautiful women, were first developed in Southern California, primarily for desert travel. Their advan-tage is that they tend to "float" over sandy terrain, providing more resistance to sinking, and they also give better steering control in sand. They are fine tires for certain conditions, but not for every-thing, as some tire makers claim. They are good on sand, natur-

154

ally, and on some kinds of mud. Gumbo, for instance, isn't one of their fortes, because gumbo is so greasy. A good gumbo tire digs in and bites into the ground; big, wide flotation tires tend to spin on top. On the other hand, big tires are fantastic for river-fording and creek-jumping, and no one should really travel wet gumbo anyway. Gumbo is best handled by chains on narrower tires, making deep ruts deeper and causing every driver following, when the road dries, to use some wicked language, and perhaps even violence, if you're ever found.

Snow is best handled by narrower tires, too. One reason especially pertinent to the plains is that narrower tires rob you of less power in crusted snow. Another reason is that snow, like gumbo, is most effectively traversed by tires that dig in and bite; I haven't yet seen snow that would "float" a vehicle. Oh, for a little ways, maybe — but that can be worse than none at all. A wide-tired vehicle, for instance, will often carry you farther out across a drifted area, leaving you in deeper snow when your vehicle finally, and inevitably, sinks.

Big tires are also expensive to buy chains for, and chains are an essential requirement for snow. Not that they're needed all the time, but they can come in handy. Like any other tool, their judicious use is imperative. Someone who chains up all four wheels on his Blazer and attempts to blast his way through a crusted coulee will wind up with a severe problem. The chains in that situation will probably just get you in deeper.

Some four-wheel-drive users claim that the only proper place for a single set of chains is on the front end of the vehicle. This can be true if steering control is needed, but it will also put stress on your hubs, and since the engine is in the front, the tendency is for a vehicle to dig the front end down into snow.

I carry one or two sets of chains, not because I feel I must go everywhere, but because they can help get me out of certain situations. Snow conditions, for one thing, can change drastically over a day, and the road you traveled in the morning just by slipping into four-wheel may be impossible without chains in the afternoon. Also, if you do get stuck in four-wheel, what do you do? Sometimes you can dig your way out, but sometimes you can't. A high-lift jack and a set of chains can get you out of almost anything four-wheel-drive gets you into. Just jack up each wheel and chain it.

Because I seem to be one of the most fallible of a fallible species, I'll give you a good example of what not to do when hunting in snow and let you take it from there. A couple of falls ago I was hunting on a ranch where a cousin was working. I'd left my four-wheel-drive with my wife, assured that we could use one of the ranch four-wheels for hunting. The vehicle we used was a one-ton flatbed truck with big wide tires on it, since it was used for feeding cattle in often-muddy fields. We didn't check to see if it had a decent jack, and none of the chains at the ranch would fit the big tires. Anyway, we were driving along a sidehill road on four inches of snow 15 miles from the nearest sign of civilization when we just slipped off the road. The rear tires went off first, and since we couldn't drive back onto the road, even in four-wheel, we had to back off into the sagebrush. We had nothing, *nothing*, in that vehicle to give us any help, and that worthless piece of junk kept slipping and sliding. Each time we'd make a run to get over the shoulder of the road, we'd end up in a more precarious position, because the road edged closer and closer to a steep coulee. Finally, after about an hour of trying different runs at the hill, we made it back up on the road and headed for the ranch, two thoroughly chastened hunters.

One last word on open-country driving: a basic rule is to stick to the ridges whenever possible. They are leveler, drier, and have less snow than coulees.

Accessories

Aside from the all-useful high-lift jack and shovel, there are a few more basic items that make traveling on the plains much more certain. Chains have been mentioned, but I'll point out that they should be tried on your tires to make sure they fit, not just bought and stuffed behind the seat. The place to try them for fit is in your driveway, not some cold ridge.

Chains also occasionally require spare pieces, like links and maybe a couple of cross-pieces, and tools to repair them. Broken chains are as worthless as those that don't fit.

A pulling chain with hooks at both ends is handy, but even better is one of the new stretch-type vehicle pullers. The prototypes of these were developed from the "rubber bands" that catch jets landing on aircraft carriers. I first encountered one

156

several years ago, in the desert sagebrush country around Fort Peck Reservoir. My wife and I and her grandparents had just spent a couple of days fishing on the lake and were driving along a sandy track heading for the nearest highway when we found our way blocked by a pickup. On getting out and investigating, we found the driver slumped over his steering wheel, the alcohol fumes telling us he was probably safer sleeping than driving. We finally brought him around enough to move his vehicle. We all got back in our pickup and started away, but as we left, I noticed that instead of merely backing off to the side to let us pass, he'd somehow managed to park his truck in a four-foot-deep gully.

So we stopped again and went back to help. I figured he'd need a wrecker to get out of that hole, but he wobbled to the back of his pickup and dragged out a long, dull-green "rope" and insisted that we hook our vehicle onto his and drive away "like nuthin' was behind ya." At this Ben looked doubtful, but finally acquiesced, mostly to get the drunk out of his hair. Ben drove away at a good clip, and as the "rope" stretched, it acted like a huge rubber band and jerked the pickup out of the gully.

"Ropes" of that type are now being manufactured and are commercially available through off-road and hunting vehicle firms. They have an enormous advantage over standard "log chains" used for pulling vehicles because you can give them a healthy jerk, something which often breaks a non-stretching chain.

Winches and come-alongs, standard equipment in many parts of the country, are not so useful on the plains as in areas with more vegetation, because there's not much you can hook them to. Some drivers carry an anchoring system that can be driven into the ground, but that's pretty hard to do in frozen or rocky ground. If you feel deprived without a winch, buy one, but don't expect it to be incredibly useful unless another vehicle is along that you can hook up to.

Aside from the normal off-road driver's assortment of spare parts, there are other items that make plains hunting easier. I mentioned that Ben Burshia and I have used short sections of stout lumber to make little "bridges" over washouts. Two-by-eight lumber not over three feet long is usually adequate; longer pieces must be thicker, and two pieces of two-inch-thick lumber bolted or screwed together are stronger than one single thicker piece.

A section of stout rope, 50 to 200 feet long, can be handy. Mine has been used mostly for hauling deer out of coulees; it is surprising how heavy a 120-pound whitetail gets when you try to muscle it up a steep, rosebush-covered slope. A trailer ball or bolt-on hook makes a good base for your rope (and for a tow rope, for that matter), and a noose around a big game animal's neck makes short work of deer hauling.

An ax and saw are also handy, mostly for cutting sagebrush or other brush to stuff under stuck vehicles' tires, sometimes necessary for traction in wet weather.

Perhaps the best item of all is some sort of large chest or toolbox that can be firmly bolted down. You need someplace to put all your junk, where it won't be sliding on top of you every time you drive downhill.

Camping

The big problem in plains camping is water — there just isn't a reliable source. Occasionally springs can be found that are pure and palatable, but too often they're tainted with alkali and even if drinkable can cause intestinal problems like diarrhea. Unless I know I'm going to be camping somewhere near a spring or freshwater lake, I haul my own H_2O. A good rule of thumb is a gallon per day per person, which usually is plenty. You can halve that in cooler weather (or bring your liquid as pop, beer, or whatever), but a half-gallon a day is skimpy for comfortable camping.

Purifying tablets are a good idea, too, even if you are near a lake, because most Western waters are used by cattle, or cattle land drains into them. Even if the water looks and tastes wonderful, it's likely to be polluted. The only water I'll drink straight on the prairie is that from a non-alkaline spring or deep-water well.

Tents should be able to withstand strong winds and have enough room to keep gear out of the elements. A tarp or fly that can be erected for shade is a must early in the season, as temperatures on even the northern plains can run into the 80's well into September. Nights can also be pretty cool; I've camped in freezing temperatures in late August in southern Saskatchewan, so fall-weight sleeping bags are recommended for northern areas.

158

Firewood can be a problem if you're out in sagebrush, and even if you aren't. Sage is full of creosote and doesn't help the flavor of your food, unless its old driftwood which has had the creosote leached out by water and sun. I've cooked many a sage driftwood meal by the shores of Fort Peck Reservoir. If you want heat or more than a minimal cooking fire anywhere on the plains, you'll usually have to rely on gas or propane, unless you're camped along a fair-sized river where cottonwood deadfalls are abundant.

No matter how barren the country, there are always varmints like skunks and 'coons to get into food left lying around. Coolers full of food and ice are best left in open shade during the day, as the inside of a vehicle will melt the ice quickly, but at night,when critters are out, it's best to lock coolers inside a car. Inside a tent, they're likely to attract the hungry. Though not dangerous like a high-country grizzly, a skunk does pose certain problems. Even if you're sleeping in a camper, you might have some close encounters of the varmint kind; Ben Burshia was once kept up all night by skunks snuffling around his camper shell. I've been kept up by a raccoon crunching chokecherries next to the tent.

First aid and snakebite kits are necessities. I've been told by many people that there aren't any rattlers north of the Montana Missouri and haven't ever run across any, but I don't take any chances. They're common in many areas farther south. It is good to have sunburn ointment early in the season, or even later if there's bright sun on snow, and insect repellent is an absolute necessity before the first hard frosts.

Be careful not to camp in a dry wash, either. Flash floods occur more often on the southern plains, but I've seen a September Montana rainfall that had water dancing two inches deep on the curved top of an asphalt road. That's a hard rain; combine that with the unporous soil of the prairies, and you're apt to get sudden creeks. Usually the best place to camp is on the side of a slight hill, where the breeze will keep the heat and insects away, but where you're out of the real ridge-top winds. Small trees for shade are a bonus, but have a perverse way of growing around watercourses, which attract floods and insects, and if they're too tall, they attract lightning, a common phenomenon on the high plains in early fall, and one to avoid.

Take a camera and color film, too, not only for your hunting triumphs but for the most incredible sunsets on earth. There's no way you'll ever catch the full impact of a major plains sunset on film, but it's fun trying.

Index

Alberta 31, 64, 70-71, 81, 82, 130, 132
archery 49-50

badlands and
  mule deer 26, 27, 31
  pheasants 81
  pronghorn 18
  whitetailed deer 5-6
bighorn sheep 33
buffalo 32-33
Bureau of Reclamation 17
Burshia, Ben 3, 4, 25, 51, 63, 78, 123, 135,
  149, 151-152, 159

California 57, 81
camping 158-160
Canada 23, 74, 130, 131
Colorado 7, 11, 23, 31, 57, 82, 88, 89, 98,
  133, 141
Corps of Engineers 17, 29-30
cranes, sandhill 141

deer, mule
  and water 29, 30-31
  boat hunting 30-31
  habitat 25, 26-27, 30-31
  intelligence 26
  rifles for 46-49
  spotting 27-28
  where to hunt 31

deer, whitetail
  habitat 3-4, 5-6, 7
  open country hunting 3-7
  plains subspecies 2
  rifles for 46-49
  timber hunting 7-10
  where to hunt 10-11
dogs
  Brittany 101
  flushing 105
  Hungarian partridge 103
  in hot weather 106
  Labrador 101
  pheasant 102, 103
  pointing 102, 103, 105
  prairie chicken 105
  quail 102
  sage grouse 105, 106
  sharptailed grouse 105
  Viszla 58, 59
dove, mourning
  guns for 138
  habitat 136-137
  shooting 137-138
  speed of flight 138
  where to hunt 138-139
driving problems
  cattle trails 151-152, 154

grass 151
gumbo 154-155
sand 154
snow 150, 154, 156
water 153-154
watercourses 151-152

Elk 33

Fort Peck Reservoir 14, 17, 23, 33, 98, 130, 132
grouse, sage
    diet 54
    dogs for 105, 106
    flight 56
    habitat 55
    size 54
    where to hunt 57
grouse, sharptailed
    diet 60
    dogs for 105
    habitat 60-62
    shooting 109-110, 117
    where to hunt 64-65

Iowa 71, 75, 89, 132, 133
Idaho 23, 71, 57, 81, 89

Kansas 11, 23, 31, 65, 75, 81, 85, 87, 88, 89, 133, 138

Manitoba 64, 71, 134, 141
Minnesota 65, 71, 143
Missouri River 31, 64, 89, 93, 126, 132, 133
Montana 7, 10, 23, 31, 33, 57, 64, 70-71, 75, 82, 97-98, 132, 141

Nebraska 7, 10-11, 23, 64, 65, 75, 81, 89, 98, 132, 133
Nevada 71
New Mexico 11, 23, 65, 81, 88, 89, 98, 134, 138, 141, 142
North Dakota 10, 23, 31, 33, 57, 64, 70-71, 82, 93, 126, 132

O'Connor, Jack 121
Oklahoma 7, 23, 31, 33, 65, 81, 87, 85, 89, 93, 133, 136, 138, 141, 142
Oregon 23, 57, 71, 81, 89

partridge, Hungarian
    dogs for 103
    flight 68-69
    habitat 67-70
    pseudonyms 70
    where to hunt 70-71

pheasant, ringnecked
    dogs for 77, 102
    drives 76-77
    habitat 75, 78-81
    where to hunt 81-82
pronghorn
    and sagebrush 20-21
    as food 21-22
    boat hunting 17-18
    eyesight 14, 18-19
    "flagging" 19
    habitat 20-21
    horse hunting 18
    speed 15
    stalking 16
    where to hunt 22-23

quail, bobwhite
    dogs for 102
    habitat 85-86
    shooting 87
    where to hunt 89
quail, scaled 88
    where to hunt 89

rabbits and hares
    cottontail 146
    jack 47, 147
    snowshoe 146
rails, sora and Virginia 142
Rau, Ron 70
rifles
    accuracy 39-40
    actions 40-41
    buffalo 33
    deer 48-49
    elk 33
    pronghorn 44-45
    sheep 33
    sighting 37-39
    small game 145, 146-147

Saskatchewan 10, 31, 33, 64, 71, 81, 82, 130, 131, 141
scope sights
    for deer rifles 49
    for pronghorn rifles 45
    for small game rifles 146
shooting, big game
    judging range 41-43
    judging wind ??
shooting, birds
    doves 138
    Hungarian partridge 116-117, 119

162

pheasant 119-120
prairie chicken 119
quail 87
sage grouse 120
sharptailed grouse 109-110, 119
shotguns
actions 112-115
chokes and loads 115-118, 138
for cranes 141
for waterfowl 131
gauges 110-112
shooting techniques 121-123, 137-138
snipe, common or Wilson's 141-142
squirrels
fox 145
gray 145-146

Texas 7, 11, 23, 31, 65, 81, 89, 93, 98, 126, 136
turkeys
calling 94-95
guns for 95-97
habitat 93
where to hunt 97-98

Utah 23, 57, 81

Vehicles
accessories 152-153, 155, 156-158
four-wheel-drive 150, 155, 156
tires 154-155

Washington (state of) 57, 71, 81, 89
waterfowl
decoys 128-131
ducks, mallards 126, 130, 133
ducks, pintail 127
ducks, teal 127
field hunting 130
geese, Canada 130, 132, 133
geese, Ross's 132
geese, snows and blues 132, 134
geese, whitefront 132
jump-shooting 127-128
lake hunting 130-131
pit blinds 124, 130
river hunting 128-129
shooting and guns 130
where to hunt 131-134
Waterman, Charles 88
Weaver, Bill 121
Wyoming 10-11, 17, 22-23, 31, 57, 64, 70-71, 82, 98, 133, 135, 137, 138, 141